Boxing From Chump to Champ

*A Beginner's Guide to Boxing Training.
Learn Self-Defense, Get Fit and Boost Your
Confidence*

Andrew Hudson

Copyright 2025 - All rights reserved.

The work contained herein has been produced with the intent to provide relevant knowledge and information on the topic described in the title for entertainment purposes only. While the author has gone to every extent to furnish up to date and true information, no claims can be made as to its accuracy or validity as the author has made no claims to be an expert on this topic. Notwithstanding, the reader is asked to do their own research and consult any subject matter experts they deem necessary to ensure the quality and accuracy of the material presented herein.

This statement is legally binding as deemed by the Committee of Publishers Association and the American Bar Association for the territory of the United States. Other jurisdictions may apply their own legal statutes. Any reproduction, transmission, or copying of this material contained in this work without the express written consent of the copyright holder shall be deemed as a copyright violation as per the current legislation in force on the date of publishing and subsequent time thereafter. All additional works derived from this material may be claimed by the holder of this copyright.

The data, depictions, events, descriptions, and all other information forthwith are considered to be true, fair, and accurate unless the work is expressly described as a work of fiction. Regardless of the nature of this work, the Publisher is exempt from any responsibility of actions taken by the reader in conjunction with this work. The Publisher acknowledges that the reader acts of their own accord and releases the author and Publisher of any responsibility for the observance of tips, advice, counsel, strategies, and techniques that may be offered in this volume.

Table of Contents

Introduction 6
    Chump Recovery 10
    My Story 15

1.1 The Basics 21
    Common Misconceptions 28
    Boxing Training 35

1.2 Preparation for Boxing 44
    Stretching 46
    Fitness 50
    Nutrition 53
    Equipment 60

1.3 Building Your Stance 66
    Orthodox 74
    Southpaw 76

1.4 Footwork Fundamentals 79
    The Methods of Movement 82
    The Body Mechanics of Footwork 95

1.5 Throwing Punches Properly 101
    Punching Techniques 105
    Basic Combinations 129

1.6 Defending Yourself 132
    Your First Line of Defense 135
    When You Can No-Longer Run 141

2.1 Improving Your Boxing Ability 173
2.2 Footwork Exercises 176
Footwork Drills 178
Ropes and Ladders 188
2.3 Punching Drills 197
Shadowboxing 198
Bag Work 205
2.4 Defensive Drills 211
Reaction Time Drills 213
Conditioning 218
Defensive Shadowboxing 225
Defensive Bag Work 232
1-On-1 Training 239
2.5 Getting Results 253
Boxing for Fitness 258
Boxing for Self-Defense 266
Boxing for Competition 272
3.1 Self-Awareness 281
How to Develop Self-Awareness 282
3.2 Changing Your Identity 289
Identity-Based Habits 295
3.3 Understanding Confidence 298
How to Make Confidence-Building a Habit 300
3.4 Pushing Your Limits 303

How to Develop Discipline... 307
How to Develop Realistic Habits That Won't Break 308

3.5 Overcoming Setbacks 310
Keeping Track of Your Setbacks 312

3.6 Strength in Numbers...................................... 313
Why We're Better in a Team 314

3.7 Champions Mentality 316
Developing a Strong Sense of Self 318

Conclusion 322

References 324

Introduction

"You don't have to be in a boxing ring to be a great fighter. As long as you are true to yourself, you will succeed in your fight for greatness." - Muhammad Ali

In basic military training, it is fairly common for recruits to participate in regular boxing training. Not because the instructors find it funny to see the troops get their asses handed to them, but because boxing training is seen as appropriate to help these men develop their self-defense skills, fitness ability, and confidence. All being crucial attributes for a soldier.

The military has no time for chumps. Soldiers have to earn their place to serve by completing basic military training, while the training differs around the world, its purpose is to push all recruits to their limits in many ways to prepare them for combat, the military tends to live by the motto "train hard, fight easy."

Boxing also has no time for chumps. Boxers need to earn their place in the gym, let alone the ring, and they get there with boxing training. Boxing training is the process that prepares boxers to fight in a squared circle. It is a combination of technical skill drills and conditioning that typically transforms weak, lazy, and timid boys into strong, confident, and brave men. You could see it as the chump-to-champ transformation.

So both soldiers and boxers are pretty tough because their training is tough, why does that matter to you? Well, as human motivation is moving away from pain and towards pleasure, more and more men are suffering the consequences of missing out on training. These men go through their life without any real challenge and ultimately this lack of struggle turns men into chumps.

A chump can mean many things, an inexperienced fighter, a fool, or somebody who's easily beaten. I like to define a chump as a man who suffers from low self-esteem: a condition characterized by a negative perception of oneself, accompanied by feelings of inadequacy, worthlessness, and a lack of confidence in one's abilities and value as a person.

Chumps struggle because they don't feel comfortable with who they are. Their lack of confidence is a result of them not having the stack of evidence that supports who they say they are. For example, having no fighting experience means feeling vulnerable in combat situations. Having no dating experience means feeling unattractive and worthless. So, if all it takes for men to boost their self-esteem is to gain experience in the area of life they feel inadequate, why do so many men still suffer?

Fear prevents men from gaining the experience they need. For example, you may not start boxing because you are worried about getting humiliated in your first session. You may not approach that attractive girl because you are worried about getting rejected. Fear is always prevalent and unfortunately, fear cannot be eliminated; it is a fundamental human emotion that will always be present when a perceived danger, threat, or harm is possible. But fear isn't the issue, not facing your fears is. You are not born a chump; it is only when you make it a habit to avoid your fears when your self-esteem plummets. The classic behaviors of chumps include:

- *Always seeking approval.*
- *Avoiding conflict.*
- *Hiding their insecurities.*
- *Always taking the easy option.*

This leads to chumps living an unsatisfying life. It is difficult to maintain relationships when you feel the need to hide who you are; it is hard to deter bullies when you don't stick up for yourself, and you're not going to get the body you want if you are put off by the training being 'too difficult'. Chumps are often stuck in a cycle, a loop of suffering.

1. Living an unsatisfying life.

2. Discovering a way to break free from an unsatisfying life.

3. Worrying about the negative outcome that may occur when trying that new method.

4. Not trying the method.

5. Repeat.

Do you want to follow that loop for the rest of your life? Of course not, use this step-by-step guide to quit being a chump. Your mental health struggles can be fixed as long as you take action on the information provided in this guide, plus you'll become a decent boxer also!

Chump Recovery

Alex, a 17-year-old kid from Salford, stepped into my boxing gym for the first time a few years back. He was 6 feet tall, skinny build, wearing clothes that I imagine his mom said he would grow into, and his most alarming feature was his swollen black eye.

I approached him and asked how I could help. He was nervous and told me with a trembling voice that he wanted to get revenge on the boys who beat him up after school. I took him to a quiet area of the gym to chat with him. I told him that boxing isn't a place to use violence and get your own back; however, I didn't turn him away because I could feel his pain.

After just a 10-minute chat with Alex, I could tell he was a chump. He was quiet; he got bullied, he didn't have a great support system around him, he lacked confidence, and it is fair to say he couldn't fight his way out of a wet paper bag. He also told me that he has been wanting to start boxing for 2 years but was scared. He reminded me of my younger self. At the end of our chat, I just asked him for one favor. I asked him to come to 3 boxing sessions and tell me at the end of each session if he still wanted to get revenge on those boys.

Alex got started and struggled to learn the basics, as did everyone, but he got frustrated very quickly. He would throw his gloves on the floor after making a mistake, he would complain when he couldn't keep up with the training and he left his first session 20 minutes early. When he left early, just before he stormed out the door, I said, "Alex I knew you couldn't handle this!"

Three days later, he came back with his own gloves, and his attitude for learning significantly improved. He asked many questions, attempted to outwork all the other boxers and he started to show signs of a smile on his face. As the months went by, he really got to grips with the basics. He built a fair bit of muscle and most importantly I could sense the confidence in him. He enjoyed each session, even the conditioning focused ones.

Alex and I are still in contact with each other today. He has recently got married to the love of his life and just like he's been doing for years; he is punching! Alex, if you're reading this, thank you. You showed me how being a coach can shape lives and although I felt bad for giving you a lot of "character building" in your first session, I'm glad I did it. So, let's get into chump recovery because it may be something you need.

Chumps live an unsatisfying life because they don't face their fears, agreed? So, what causes these fears in the first place? Genetics play a large role, as do bad past experiences, and so on, but the main thing that keeps chumps weak is their beliefs. They believe that:

- *Combat sports are "dangerous."*
- *Men should always be "good" and they'll be liked.*
- *Men should always be "right" and they'll get rewarded.*

Boys develop these ways of thinking when growing up due to lacking a father figure, having abusive parents, childhood abandonment experiences, or toxic shame. Essentially, chumps didn't have the correct role model to show them how to become a man. This all started after the Second World War, most men were forced to leave their families to serve their country and most women had to step up to be fathers to their children as well as mothers.

I am not putting women to blame here; they only raised their boys on what they thought they wanted them to be. They didn't want their little boys fighting; they wanted their boys to always be good and always do the right thing. This caused a surge in boys growing up into soft men, and as time has passed, these beliefs have become a societal norm. More on this to be discussed in further chapters.

The lessons, advice, and training presented to you in this guide are exactly what I teach to beginner boxers to give them the best start possible. Boxing is tough; it will get you down and you will want to give up, but I assure you that if you just stick with it, the results will come and your life will significantly improve. I have split this guide into 3 sections.

Section One: Learn Boxing Techniques

The aim of this guide is to teach you how to box at a beginner level, therefore in the first section, you will find instructions on how to build your strong stance, how to correctly step and move around the ring, how to throw each punch properly and finally how to use defensive techniques to keep your vulnerable areas protected.

Section Two: Improve Your Skills

The only way to become better at anything is to practice. This section contains many drills you can try at home to work on your footwork, punching, and defense. Anybody can complete the drills provided, some require equipment which is listed with the exercise. At the end of this section, we discuss how to adjust your boxing training to get you the results you desire.

Section Three: Build Confidence

The greatest attribute I gained from boxing training is confidence, therefore in the final section, we cover many strategies you can use along with regular boxing training to build ever-lasting confidence. You can also find methods to develop your self-discipline and resilience as well, crucial attributes for personal success.

My Story

With all the talking I've been doing, I have yet to introduce myself properly. My name is Andrew Hudson. I have been studying boxing and human behaviors for many years; I have also been fortunate enough to host my own boxing sessions and I have spent most of my time teaching the basics to beginners. I have absolutely loved working with chumps, here's why...

As a teenager, I was a chump and suffered because of it. I followed the previous beliefs we spoke about to a T. I would always be too nice to everybody and get stepped on. I feared speaking to girls, and I was addicted to junk food and anything that brought me quick comfort. I was just a fat, spotty kid who never got what he wanted; and I hated every minute of it.

I had always been interested in boxing training. I noticed that boxers are in good shape and get all the ladies - which was a huge motivator for young Andrew. I went to my first session expecting to leave the session with a much better body and great fighting ability, oh how I was wrong. I left the session feeling angry and exhausted, I couldn't keep up with the other boxers and the coach didn't even let me punch the bag.

I didn't want to return, but I started to realize that if I couldn't even complete one session, then how was I going to achieve anything in my life? So I forced myself to go to 2 sessions a week. It was tough, but for the first time in my life, I felt as if I had accomplished something. I kept going back, my mood was improving, I became more comfortable with speaking to others, my flabby chest became less flabby and I could finally punch a heavy bag. The more I boxed, the more I loved boxing. As my mood improved, I wanted to understand why, so I took up reading and built a small habit of studying psychology each day.

Fast forward to today, I have helped hundreds of people quit being a chump. I love helping people, and I fully understand how people can change for the good. I have witnessed scared, weak, and unfit men turn their lives around and become much stronger individuals because they took up boxing and followed my instructions. Going from Chump to Champ!

As much as I enjoy coaching people face-to-face, it is hard to find time to help everyone. That is why I have spent a few years publishing books to help a wider audience.

I genuinely want to make you better physically, mentally, and emotionally. I am confident it will happen once you take action on the lessons in this guide, the sport I love so dear. I may be a little biased here, but boxing helps people in every aspect of their lives, in a way that other activities or sports can't. With physicality, pain, mental toughness, tenacity, and intelligence involved, very few things out there can compare to the sweet science.

I have written this book as if it was for my younger self, a young Andrew who didn't like reading and wasn't easily motivated, therefore the information is simple to understand and you'll find plenty of encouragement throughout. Reading doesn't help anybody until the instructions are put into action!

Your greatest comeback is in the making, but for this to happen you need to take action. Nobody can get better by thinking about doing something, they get better by doing. Whether you want to build up a basic boxing ability and feel confident enough to join a gym, or you want to stop being a wimp, or you just want a fun boxing workout, I hope this guide serves you well. Finally, please consult with a doctor before training. Your health is always the number one priority.

The Boxing Training Handbook

A summary of essential boxing teachings, combining physical training techniques, practical drills, and key psychological lessons, in clear and concise points.

Follow the link below to download the handbook for **free**

www.subscribepage.io/boxingtraining

The Confidence Workbook

A hands-on guide containing 7 simple strategies designed to help you build self-esteem and develop confidence today.

Follow this link to get your **free** online copy

subscribepage.io/buildconfidence

Section One: Learn Boxing Techniques

1.1 The Basics

1.2 Preparation for Boxing

1.3 Building Your Stance

1.4 Footwork Fundamentals

1.5 Throwing Punches Properly

1.6 Defending Yourself

1.1 The Basics

"Success is neither magical nor mysterious. Success is the natural consequence of consistently applying the basic fundamentals." - E. James Rohn

Boxing is a combat sport that involves two opponents engaging in a regulated bout within a defined area, typically a square ring. The primary objective of boxing is to land punches on the opponent while avoiding or blocking their punches, with the ultimate goal of scoring points or achieving a knockout to win the match.

Boxing matches are governed by a set of rules and regulations which are very similar around the world. The boxers sign contracts before their fights which dictate the length of rounds, the number of rounds, the weight class, and many other variables. The fights are scored by judges and the referee enforces the rules throughout the fight. The standard rules for professional boxing are:

- The ring must meet certain specifications, usually between 16-20 feet on each side.

- Rounds are normally 3 minutes long with a 1-minute rest between. The number of rounds depends on the level—the maximum is 12.

- Points are scored by judges at the end of each round on a 10-point scale. It is common for rounds to end 10-9, causing the boxer with 10 to win the round. A boxer loses a point when they are knocked down, when they get hurt significantly, or if they foul—this is down to the judge's decision.

- Fouls can end in a boxer losing a point or being disqualified. Fouls include hitting below the belt, headbutting, holding, excessive clinching, hitting an opponent who is down, and using elbows or knees.

Boxing is a very popular sport; it has millions of participants and fans worldwide and has been around for thousands of years. The origins of boxing can be traced back to ancient civilizations in Egypt and Greece, hand-to-hand combat has always been a common form of competition and entertainment. Throughout its long history, boxing has undergone significant changes and adaptations, but its essence as a test of strength, skill, and endurance remains constant.

Boxing is never the case of just showing up and hoping for the best. You must prepare for each fight to the best of your ability with countless hours of intense training. With each fight, the boxers' reputation, health, and well-being are on the line, therefore anybody who steps into the ring is automatically respected.

Plenty of people like to criticize boxers from their living room sofa but they have no idea how difficult it is to fight in the ring. To be a great boxer, you need a high level of stamina, muscular endurance, strength, power, courage, agility, bravery, intelligence, and composure to perform in front of a crowd. Let's take a look at some of the boxing greats.

Muhammed Ali. In my opinion, the greatest ever. He was much more than just a boxer; he was a cultural icon, a social activist, and one of the most significant athletes of the 20th century. Renowned for his lightning-fast footwork, dazzling hand speed, and unparalleled charisma, Ali transcended the sport of boxing to become a global symbol of strength, resilience, and social justice. He captured the heavyweight championship 3 times and holds the record of 56 wins, 5 losses, and 37 knockouts.

"Float like a butterfly, sting like a bee."

Floyd Mayweather Jr. is widely regarded as one of the greatest boxers of all time. Known for his exceptional defensive skills, tactical brilliance, and unbeaten professional record, Mayweather earned the nickname "Money" for his ability to generate massive pay-per-view revenue and for his lavish lifestyle outside the ring. He holds an impressive record of 50 wins, 0 losses, and 27 knockouts, he captured world titles in multiple weight classes and his ability to hit and not be hit was very frustrating for his opponents.

"A true champion can adapt to anything."

Tyson Fury. Standing at 6 feet 9 inches tall, Fury possesses a rare combination of agility, speed, and technical ability for a heavyweight boxer. He has openly discussed his struggles with mental health issues, addiction, and his journey to redemption, becoming an advocate for mental health awareness and inspiring many with his resilience and openness. At the time of writing this he holds the record of 34 wins, and 0 losses and has held heavyweight titles for many years.

"People can say what they want about me. But I've got a big heart and will keep going."

It is clear to see how the greatest boxers of all time would benefit from boxing, money, fame, women, and so on. What's in it for the average Joe? I mean, boxing is mentally challenging, physically demanding, and fairly intimidating, and each time you step into that ring you could face possible public humiliation and reputational damage. Why should anybody in their right mind box?

It isn't as bad as you may think. Boxing offers a range of physical, mental, and emotional benefits to those to stick to it. Here are some of the key advantages of regular boxing training:

- **Enhanced Mood**: If you try a boxing session right now, I guarantee that you will feel much better about yourself after completing the session compared to how you feel right now. The physical exertion and focus required in boxing can act as a form of stress relief, helping to reduce tension and improve mood by releasing endorphins, the body's natural feel-good chemicals. Furthermore, regular boxing training improves cognitive function and brain health.

- **Improved Body Composition**: We all want to look good and boxing training helps you do just that. Boxing is a whole-body workout that helps you build muscle and burn fat, as it contains such a wide variety of bodyweight exercises and training methods. Each boxing session helps you burn plenty of calories, very helpful for weight management, plus how many boxers have you seen with beer bellies? (excluding Andy Ruiz)

- **Improved Cardiovascular Health**: Boxing involves intense cardiovascular workouts, which can improve your heart health, endurance, and overall fitness levels. Boxers are very fit and typically maintain great energy levels.

- **Enhanced Strength and Muscular Endurance**: The repetitive punching, footwork, bodyweight exercises, and defensive movements in boxing help you build strength and muscle tone, particularly in the arms, shoulders, core, and legs.

- **Boosted Self-Esteem**: Learning and mastering boxing techniques can boost self-esteem, as boxers gain a sense of accomplishment and improve their physical abilities. The more you train, the better you become and you build a stack of evidence that you are good at boxing—eliminating any doubts you may have started with.

- **Discipline and Focus**: In boxing, you must adhere to training schedules, follow instructions from coaches, and stay committed to improving skills. By completing regular boxing training your ability to push yourself and stick with difficult habits significantly improves.

- **Self-Defense Skills**: Boxing teaches valuable self-defense techniques, helping you feel more confident and capable of protecting yourself or loved ones in threatening situations.

- **Boxing is Fun**: There aren't many workouts where you get to punch your problems away. Boxing workouts have so much scope to what can be trained as a boxer needs to be well rounded in all areas of their boxing and fitness ability, therefore it is unlikely to repeat the exact same sessions over and over.

Common Misconceptions

Boxing has gained a relatively bad reputation throughout the years. Many people dislike the sport because they see the professionals as bad role models, some people see it as a place for bullies to be violent to newcomers, and some think that you are obliged to fight in the ring the second you join a gym. The fall in boxing's reputation is the result of dodgy rumors and incorrect beliefs.

Sure, there are a few professional boxers who paint a bad picture of the sport and there are certainly a few gyms around the world that will bully the newcomers—however, you cannot let the few outliers ruin the entire sport.

The world is evolving towards a softer stance. There is a worry about an entitlement culture, especially among younger generations, where success is expected without effort. Modern parenting and societal norms are accused of coddling the younger generation, shielding them from adversity. This overprotection may leave kids ill-equipped for real-world challenges. Finally, the world is moving towards instant gratification due to improved technology, social media, and so on. It's getting to the point where needs and desires can be fulfilled very quickly without much effort.

More and more men struggle each day because life for most of us is becoming more comfortable. Boxing certainly isn't a comfortable experience which is why fewer men are willing to give it a go—instead, they spend hours on TikTok each day while eating calorie-dense foods. Our brains are wired to crave the quick and easy rewards, so of course that stuff is addictive.

There is a severe lack of struggle in most men's lives, although I am not encouraging you to throw your life away to live in the wild like a tribesman, please understand that the main reason why your life sucks right now is because you always pick the easiest option. If you are one of those men who wants to get in shape and learn how to box, but won't go to a boxing session because it seems too difficult, seriously take some time to understand you cannot expect a different output from the same input.

Below, you can find the Big 3 common misconceptions of boxing training debunked. You will soon realize that boxing isn't as bad as it sounds. At the end of the day, everything in life has its negative views, so it's up to you to decide whether boxing is for you or not.

Misconception 1: Boxing Training Is Dangerous

Yes, boxing training can be dangerous if you don't wear protective gear like hand wraps or boxing gloves. It can also be dangerous if you decide to throw punches with improper form or attempt to fight the best boxer in the gym for some kind of ego boost. Below is what you should expect on your first session.

When you go to your first boxing session, it is likely you will chat with the coach first before getting started. They will ask about your past boxing experience and what you want to achieve from boxing training, they may also introduce you to the rest of the boxers. For those of you who suffer from social anxiety, you may find this part the most uncomfortable. This is an ex-chump speaking here. I had to introduce myself to around 30 boxers on my arrival. I had social anxiety when introducing myself. I was visibly nervous, sweaty, and stuttered on my words. Not one of them cared; they gave me a warm welcome.

So, boxing will not put you in any danger; unless you ignore your coaches or run your mouth to other boxers for no reason. If somebody does get hurt in boxing, everybody will stop and they receive treatment. You will probably find your first session very uncomfortable due to the fitness required to keep up with the rest—my advice is to just get on with it, because eventually you will be able to keep up.

Misconception 2: Boxing Training Is Only for Fighters

Yes, boxing training is definitely most useful for fighters, but anybody can complete a boxing session. You are not required to compete in the ring after your first boxing session. You may be encouraged to go after a few months of training if your coaches see potential in you, but you can always say no. Make it clear to your coaches what you want to do. Also, you don't even have to box at the gym. Boxing training at home allows you to get the outcomes you want from boxing without needing to fight anybody. How and where you train is up to you.

Misconception 3: You Cannot Learn How to Box from a Book

Yes, you would pick up the basic boxing techniques much quicker at a gym because gyms offer a great learning environment—however, I understand that may not be an option for you.

Many people will be quick to tell you that you simply cannot learn how to box from reading a book. Furthermore, they will add that you need to join a boxing gym to have any chance of learning the basics.

You simply cannot learn anything just from reading a book, you learn by taking action on the information provided. Therefore, you can learn the basic boxing techniques by reading this book and practicing them in your own time. You need to take action on the techniques and lessons in this book and don't worry, we will get to the teachings soon.

I will admit, the boxing gym is the best place to learn how to box. You will receive attention and help from coaches which is very useful for correcting any errors in your technique, and you will be in an environment where everybody is practicing boxing. This will be highly motivating, making you feel part of a team.

I understand that you may not want to go to a gym, maybe you feel intimidated, or maybe there isn't a gym near you, whatever the reason is just know joining a gym is not mandatory. You can definitely learn the boxing basics at home. In my opinion, the best way to learn or develop your skills is to do as many repetitions as possible, of course ensuring these repetitions are using the correct form.

"Fear not the man who has practiced 10,000 kicks once, but I fear the man who has practiced one kick 10,000 times." - Bruce Lee

Take this approach to learning boxing techniques. The man who practiced his cross 10,000 times will most certainly drop anybody who meets his fist. So, if you throw a punch 100 times and it doesn't feel right, guess what? You have at least 9,900 more repetitions to complete.

The only issue is that it is very easy to pick up small faults in your technique and it can be very difficult to recognize these flaws on your own. That is why I recommend everybody to go to a few boxing sessions when learning the basics. Having a coach correct you can seriously help develop your understanding of the techniques. I have found my best method of learning to be from making mistakes.

Yet again, it all depends on the results you want from boxing training. If you just box for fitness, a small error in your jab won't be problematic, whereas it could be a huge weakness that your opponent could expose in a competitive fight.

Boxing Training

Boxing training is simply how boxers prepare for their next fight. To be a great boxer, you need to be fast, powerful, intelligent, technical, agile, and mentally tough. Boxing training is what allows you to improve each of these attributes to enhance your boxing ability.

I am sure you have watched a boxing match. You may have even claimed to be able to outbox heavyweight professionals from the comfort of your living room. I was the same growing up; I watched heavyweight boxers and criticized them for being slow, even though I couldn't fight my way out of a wet paper bag. The point is that you don't realize how difficult boxing is until you get punched in the face or train past exhaustion.

It is tough to fight in the ring, therefore the training needs to be even tougher. A boxing session typically involves a combination of cardiovascular exercises, strength and conditioning workouts, technical skill drills, sparring sessions, and mental preparation techniques.

Boxing sessions range from gym to gym. Below I have put together the typical structure of a boxing training session to give you an idea of what to expect when going to your first session or to create your own home boxing sessions.

Warm-up (10 mins)

1. Jogging or skipping rope: To increase heart rate and warm up the body.

2. Dynamic stretches and mobility exercises. To prepare muscles and joints for the workout.

3. Shadow boxing: Practicing boxing techniques without a partner, focusing on footwork, punches, and defensive movements. I like to see it as fighting an imaginary opponent.

Technique Drills (20 mins)

1. Focus mitts or pad work: Participants pair up with a partner or coach to practice punching combinations, defensive maneuvers, and counterattacks.

2. Heavy bag work: Participants work on power and technique by hitting a heavy bag and practicing various punches, combinations, and footwork.

3. Speed bag or double-end bag: Participants work on timing, coordination, and hand speed by hitting a speed bag or double-end bag.

Skill Development (20 mins)

1. Sparring (more for advanced boxers): Controlled, simulated combat with a partner to practice applying techniques in a dynamic and reactive environment.

2. Partner drills: Participants work with a partner on specific skills such as slipping punches, blocking, or clinching.

Conditioning (20 mins)

1. Interval training: High-intensity intervals of boxing-specific exercises such as punching drills, footwork drills, or circuits.

2. Bodyweight exercises: Mainly core strengthening exercises, pushups, squats and so on.

Cool Down and Stretching (10 mins)

1. Slow jogging or shadowboxing to gradually lower heart rate.

2. Static stretches targeting major muscle groups to improve flexibility and reduce muscle soreness.

3. Foam rolling or self-myofascial release to relax tight muscles and improve recovery (optional).

That is a very basic overview. Some gyms may go straight into sparring after the warmup, whereas others don't do any sparring at all. If you plan to train at home, keep this structure in mind because it will be the foundation of your future training sessions.

Boxing is not just a sport but a discipline that demands dedication, perseverance, and a commitment to continuous improvement. You cannot become good at boxing just by punching a bag every now and then; it needs serious commitment. Boxers need to be in a routine. Aside from boxing sessions, boxers stick to a strict healthy diet. Their habits should allow for proper recovery. Pretty much, boxers do everything in their power to maximize their performance on fight night.

A boxer's routine depends on the outcome they desire. A boxer looking to fight at a professional level will use every second of their time wisely to prepare for the fight, whereas somebody looking to get in shape will still pay attention to their diet and complete regular exercise—but won't feel the need to go overboard with conditioning. Now that we have covered training methods, basic routine, and other factors that go into boxing, let's look at boxing techniques.

The techniques are split into 4 sections: stance, footwork, punching, and defending. Each section has its own collection of techniques. Below are brief descriptions of each. I go into plenty more detail in their designated chapters. You will learn in these chapters how to perform the various techniques involved, what purpose they serve, when to use them, common mistakes to avoid, and much more.

Stance

The boxing stance refers to the fundamental body position that a boxer adopts during a fight or training session. It's crucial for balance, mobility, and defense, as well as for generating power in punches.

Footwork

Skillful movement and foot placement to control distance, angles, and positioning in the ring, facilitating effective offense and defense. Also maintaining proper body mechanics to ensure the most effective performance.

Punching

In boxing, a punch is a striking technique used to score points, wear down opponents, or achieve knockouts. Each punch is executed with specific mechanics and targets different areas of the opponent's body.

Defense

Defense in boxing refers to the techniques and strategies used by a boxer to avoid or minimize the impact of an opponent's punches while simultaneously protecting oneself from injury. Effective defense is crucial for survival in the ring, as it allows a boxer to withstand an opponent's attacks, counter effectively, and conserve energy.

Finally, it is a good idea to gain a decent understanding of the boxing attributes. Below is a list of physical and mental qualities that contribute to success in boxing, each attribute can be improved with regular practice.

- **Strength**: The force that allows boxers to deliver impactful punches, absorb blows, and maintain control in clinches.

- **Speed**: Quickness in both hand and foot movements, enabling boxers to deliver fast punches, evade strikes, and move swiftly around the ring.

- **Agility**: Nimbleness and flexibility are both crucial for maneuvering around opponents, ducking under punches, and maintaining balance while moving and punching.

- **Endurance**: Muscular and cardiovascular fitness to sustain high-intensity activity throughout rounds and withstand fatigue, ensuring consistent performance over the duration of a fight. Mainly improved by long-distance running.

- **Accuracy**: Precision and control in delivering punches, targeting specific areas of the opponent's body with maximum efficiency and effectiveness. Improved by bag work and 1-on-1 training.

- **Timing**: The ability to gauge the rhythm and tempo of a fight, executing punches, defenses, and movements at the opportune moment to capitalize on openings and create advantages. Improved by 1-on-1 training.

- **Reaction Time**: The ability to perceive and respond to opponents' movements and attacks, allowing for rapid evasion, counters, and defensive maneuvers. Improved by most defensive drills.

- **Durability**: Physical resilience and ability to absorb punishment, minimizing the impact of opponents' punches and recovering quickly from blows. Improved by conditioning.

- **Focus**: Mental discipline and clarity to maintain attention, focus on the task at hand, and execute strategies and tactics under pressure. Generally improved in all boxing training drills.

- **Confidence**: Self-assurance and belief in one's abilities, which is crucial for taking calculated risks, asserting dominance, and overcoming adversity in the ring. Improved by experience.

- **Mental Strength**: Mental and emotional fortitude to endure adversity, push through challenges, and remain resilient in the face of physical and mental strain. Improved by challenging yourself.

- **Intelligence**: Tactical awareness, strategic thinking, and the ability to read opponents, analyze situations, and adapt game plans accordingly. Improved by experience.

1.2 Preparation for Boxing

The fight is won or lost far away from witnesses—behind the lines, in the gym, and out there on the road, long before I dance under those lights. - Muhammad Ali

Boxing training isn't a walk in the park. It's tough because it needs to make boxers physically and mentally tough. If boxing training was easy, then how could it prepare anybody to knock out an opponent in the ring? Most of the time, the boxing match is won before the fight, the winner being whoever trained the hardest.

As this is a beginner's guide to boxing training, we will talk less about fighting and more about getting you ready for your first boxing session. Whether you plan to join a boxing gym, train with friends at home, or you just want to learn how to punch a bag properly, you must prepare yourself for the first time, and in this chapter, we cover how.

I assume that you haven't got great experience with boxing. Maybe you've never seen the inside of a boxing gym, or maybe you have never thrown a punch before! Your experience doesn't matter; I can assure you that anybody of any ability can learn the boxing basics. It's just that some people require more preparation for getting into a boxing routine than others. For example, people who have been playing sports since a young age are more likely to cope with the physical side of boxing than people who haven't got a sporting background.

In this chapter, you can discover how to prepare for your first boxing session with regular stretching, fitness tips, nutritional advice, and recommended equipment. Although many people say the best way to start boxing is to jump straight into a session. From what I have witnessed throughout my years as a boxing coach, the newbies who seriously struggle with the intensity of training don't return after their first session. Getting started is always the hardest part, so when beginners don't know what to expect or can't keep up, then it can be a huge demotivator.

I always encourage beginners to complete a simple 3-week training program at home before going to their first session. In this program, beginners build great habits for stretching, exercise, and great nutrition, which leads to a much-improved performance in their first session. I hope for these habits to stay with you for a lifetime; these small changes provide significant results.

Stretching

I have been stretching regularly for quite a while and I genuinely hate it. It's boring and uncomfortable. However, I haven't picked up a serious injury in the past 5+ years yet I feel pretty flexible and I'm also quite sharp in the ring. I have to thank stretching for that.

Boxing gets your body moving in ways you didn't even know were possible. You exercise at a high intensity and use every muscle in your body, therefore if your muscles feel tight before a workout, injury is likely. Furthermore, if you are a stiff person and an absolute embarrassment on the dancefloor, you will have more difficulty performing the techniques and movements in boxing.

Stretching, when done properly, prevents injury and improves flexibility. I recommend that you start stretching for just 5-10 minutes a day. Nothing crazy, just build that habit. The best times to stretch are before and after a workout, this is when tight muscles are more likely to be pulled, strained, or even torn. So, ensure that you include a wide variety of stretches in your warmups and cooldowns. I also recommend stretching on your days off; it helps with recovery, and building the habit is what is important here.

Most people know that stretching is important, but don't do it because they forget about it or find it uncomfortable. The best way to combat this issue is to write out your workout or daily routine and write down the stretches you must do alongside the workout so you can tick them off as you complete them. Tracking your small wins goes a long way.

We will go over some basic stretches that you can start using. Each stretch comes with a brief description of how to do it. I have covered the main muscle groups to stretch below:

- **Chest Stretch**: Stand facing forward and clasp your hands together behind your back. Now, push your chest forward. To get an even better stretch, have a partner gently push your arms together, which will open up your chest more.

- **Shoulder Stretch**: Extend one arm across your body at shoulder height. Use your opposite hand to gently pull the extended arm towards your chest until you feel a stretch in the shoulder. Stretch both shoulders.

- **Hamstrings**: Sit on the floor with one leg extended straight in front of you and the other leg bent. Keeping your back straight, hinge forward at the hips, reaching towards your toes with both hands. Hold the stretch for 15-30 seconds, then switch legs.

- **Calves**: Put the ball of your foot against the wall and push until you feel your calf muscle stretch. Do this with each foot.

- **Groin**: Sit on the floor with the soles of your feet together, allowing your knees to drop out to the sides. Hold on to your feet or ankles with your hands and gently press your knees towards the floor using your elbows. Keep your back straight and gently lean forward at the hips until you feel a stretch in the inner thighs and groin.

- **Lower Back**: Kneel on the floor with your knees hip-width apart and your toes touching. Sit back on your heels and extend your arms forward on the floor, lowering your chest towards your thighs. Rest your forehead on the floor and relax your entire body.

- **Lunges**: This particular stretch will target your hip flexor muscles. All you have to do is get into a runner's stance with one leg forward and then go into a full lunge. Perform this on each side. This will help loosen up your muscles after exercises like burpees or mountain climbers.

- **Cobra Pose**: Lay down on your stomach with the palm of your hand touching the floor on each side of your chest. Slowly push up, lifting your torso off the floor while keeping your legs down. You should feel your abdominal muscles stretching.

Feel free to add more stretches to that list, you know your body best. A few questions I recommend you think about each time after you complete your stretching routine. Could you feel the stretch in your muscles? Did you hold the stretch for long enough? Did you stretch both sides evenly? Did you notice any real pain or discomfort? Is there any way you can improve your stretching routine for next time?

Fitness

"Fatigue makes cowards of us all." - George Patton

Anybody of any fitness level can start boxing. However, you will find it much more difficult to keep up with the intensity of training if you are unfit. Therefore, to prepare for your first boxing session, take some time to work on improving your fitness ability.

I'm not going to tell you why fitness is important, you already know. Just know that if you ignore it, there will be consequences. I understand that you want to go to a boxing session to punch the bag, not to do 100 burpees. Unfortunately, you don't get to choose. You simply cannot cheat fitness as it is such an important part of the sweet science, plus punching the bag to a good standard requires a decent level of fitness anyway. So now you know what's expected of you, you may as well start working on your fitness to prepare for hell.

No matter who you are, in every boxing session you will train to exhaustion. It doesn't matter how fit or fat you are, boxing is designed to push you to your limit. Just because the fittest guy in the gym can do 50 pushups without breaking a sweat, doesn't mean he won't train to exhaustion because the coach will make him do 200.

The problem is that if you are too unfit, you are likely to hold the group behind. Nobody wants to be that guy doing kneeling push ups in a puddle of sweat 2 minutes after everybody else has finished. Trust me, being that guy in the past, it is fairly embarrassing. If you think you are too unfit for boxing, give yourself 3 weeks to do something about it. Below are some tips I encourage you to try:

1. Run. Everybody can run, so I challenge you to run the furthest distance you have ever run. Aim to do this within a week of reading this. It doesn't need to be a PB and you don't need to run 100 km. Just test yourself, and see where you are at with your fitness. If you fail, don't beat yourself up, it's better than nothing. If you are not a regular runner, I recommend setting a goal of running 5k to get started. At the end of your run, note down your distance and time, now you know what you are capable of.

2. Aim for 30 minutes of exercise 4 times a week. Now it's time to build a habit. 30 minutes of exercise a day really isn't much, and as you get into boxing, you will start to exceed this more often than not. The exercise you do is

completely up to you, running, biking, walking, sports, weight training, or even boxing at home!

3. Track and journal your exercise. After every time you exercise, take 5 minutes to track it. Ask yourself questions like, how did it go? What was the most difficult part of the exercise? How do you feel after the exercise? Have you progressed towards your goal? Do you think you could have performed better? How do you plan to make your next exercise more difficult?

4. Focus on recovery. Recovery is a bit of a complicated topic in boxing, although, yes, you need to recover properly to prevent injury and prepare for the next session, many boxers claim to have never given a toss about recovery as their only goal is to push themselves as far as possible. When getting started, I recommend paying attention to proper recovery, so here are some basic recovery tips: 8 hours of sleep a night, deep stretching after exercise, a balanced diet high in protein, staying hydrated, and not training on injuries.

Nutrition

What you eat and drink directly affects your mood, energy levels, physical performance, cognitive function, immune system function, and many other daily functions. The bottom line is: If you eat like crap, you will train like crap and also probably feel like crap. Constant poor nutrition will not only negatively impact your boxing performance but damage your career, health, relationships, and sleep patterns. Don't risk it all for a chocolate bar!

Most, if not all, athletes have their own nutritionists. They assess the dietary needs of athletes and create personalized nutrition plans to help them achieve their sport-related goals. Athletes need all the help they can get to enhance performance, so that is why you see professional boxers spending thousands on the best nutritionists. At your level, a nutritionist may not be the best move, but please acknowledge the steps below to help enhance your performance when training.

Step 1 - Understand your nutritional requirements. Consider your age, gender, weight, height, activity level, fitness goals, and any specific health considerations. The more active you are, the more calories your body needs. Women typically require fewer calories than men. If you have high muscle mass, you require more protein. Use a calorie calculator to estimate your recommended calorie intake, I recommend MyFitnessPal.

Step 2 - Understand what results you want to achieve. Do you want to lose weight, build muscle mass, improve athletic performance, or better your mental health? Be specific with your goals, plan how much weight you want to lose, or know exactly what you want to look like. Your goal determines how much you should eat, again use MyFitnessPal for help.

Step 3 - Know when to eat. It's no good eating right before a workout because you will just turn into what I call a Chunder Dragon. It is recommended to split your day of eating into 4-5 smaller meals to maintain great energy levels. Try to exercise for at least 30 minutes after eating. Drink water throughout the day and be aware that eating large meals late at night may disturb your sleeping pattern.

Step 4 - Cut down on junk food. The big 3 to avoid are fast food, sugary drinks, and processed snack foods. These foods are often high in unhealthy fats, refined carbohydrates, and sodium. They are also frequently served in large portions, contributing to excess calorie intake.

You may feel immediate satisfaction when eating junk food because it is a nice treat and our brains are programmed to crave calorie-dense foods. However, you might also experience a subsequent energy crash, feelings of guilt or regret, digestive discomfort, and increased thirst, and if you make a habit of eating junk, then look forward to long-term health effects such as obesity and chronic diseases.

It is quite unrealistic to completely cut out junk food. Your cravings for it will continue to stay present and it would be pretty robotic to never have your favorite chocolate again. Consume junk food in moderation, most definitely cut down and if you do plan on fighting in the ring, then seriously limit or cut out junk food—the more you want to get results, the stricter your diet should be.

Step 5 - Include a wide range of healthy foods in your diet. Healthy foods are nutrient-dense, meaning they provide essential vitamins, minerals, fiber, and other beneficial compounds while being relatively low in calories, unhealthy fats, added sugars, and sodium. Try to have a diet containing these foods:

- Fruit and Vegetables: They are rich in vitamins, minerals, antioxidants, and fiber. Attempt to have these with meals or for snacks. Examples include apples, berries, oranges, bananas, grapes, kiwi, and mango. Plus leafy greens, cruciferous vegetables, root vegetables, and bell peppers.

- Whole Grains: A good source of complex carbohydrates, fiber, vitamins, and minerals. They provide sustained energy and promote digestive health. Choose whole grain options such as brown rice, quinoa, oats, barley, whole wheat bread, and whole grain pasta.

- Lean Proteins: Very essential for muscle growth, repair, and overall health. They are low in saturated fat and cholesterol. Include lean protein sources such as skinless poultry, lean cuts of beef or pork, fish, tofu, tempeh, legumes, and low-fat dairy products. Make this the majority of your calorie intake.

- Healthy Fats: Important for heart health, brain function, and hormone production. Incorporate sources of unsaturated fats into your diet, such as avocados, nuts, seeds, and fatty fish.

- Dairy or Dairy Alternatives: Providing calcium, protein, and other nutrients. Choose low-fat or non-fat options like skim milk, yogurt, and cheese, or opt for dairy alternatives such as almond milk, soy milk, or coconut yogurt fortified with calcium and vitamin D.

- Nuts and Seeds: Nutrient-dense snacks that provide healthy fats, protein, fiber, vitamins, and minerals. Enjoy them as a snack on their own or add them to yogurt, salads, oatmeal, or smoothies. Examples include almonds, walnuts, chia seeds, flaxseeds, pumpkin seeds, and sunflower seeds.

- Water and Hydrating Beverages: Staying hydrated is essential for overall health and well-being. Choose water as your primary beverage and aim to drink plenty of fluids throughout the day. You can also enjoy hydrating beverages like herbal teas, infused water, and sparkling water with a splash of citrus. Aim for 3 liters of water a day.

Step 6 - Develop the willpower to stick to a healthy diet. You may already know how to eat healthy, you just can't resist taking from the cookie jar. Some tips to help you stick to a clean diet. Don't stock your cupboards with junk food. Plan a cheat meal once or twice a week. Get support from close friends or family. Understand that you will feel regret after eating junk food. Punish yourself appropriately when you cheat on your diet.

Step 7 - Build healthy habits. Yet again, habits generate results. If you eat 500 calories more than your recommended intake each day, your habit of overeating will make you gain weight. I recommend that you track your diet, even on days when you're eating goes to shit. Prepare your food for the following day, it is much easier to eat healthy when the food is ready to eat. Think before you eat, when you get tempted by junk food, ask yourself 2 questions: Will this help me achieve my goal? Will I feel good after eating this? Finally, track your progress toward your goal. This is a great habit that makes you feel confident that what you are doing is working.

So, if your diet is poor, you're weak. You are the only person who can control what you eat. Have some grit about you and start saying no to the things that are keeping you unhealthy and miserable.

There is only so much I can say about diet and nutrition. There are textbooks, websites, and all sorts of information on this subject. If you look up this information, make sure it is from a credible source. If you get serious about your boxing career, then you can get a consultation with a nutrition expert, if you wish. You certainly do not have to. Just don't eat like a fatso and you should be grand.

Equipment

It is possible to box without equipment. You only need a bit of open space to do some shadow boxing and bodyweight exercises. However, that isn't really going to help you get any results. At least you'll want some basic equipment to feel somewhat like a boxer.

Equipment is designed to offer protection and help improve boxing attributes. You might not like the idea of having to spend money on equipment, however, there are some things you might dislike more:

- *Putting your hands in the only pair of stinky spare gloves at the gym.*

- *The feeling of your wrists and knuckles almost breaking with each punch you throw.*

- *The boredom of only being able to shadowbox.*

Buy some equipment, it's an investment. Growing up, I was always very tight with my money. The only thing that encouraged me to spend money was thinking about the cost per use. For example, if you spend £150 on boxing gear and box 300 times in a year, then that's £0.50 per session, very cheap if you ask me. I recommend investing in the essential boxing equipment below:

Hand Wraps

They stabilize your wrists and hands, reducing the risk of sprains and fractures. Hand wraps are great for absorbing shock, preventing joint hyperextension, improving blood circulation, and maintaining hand hygiene by absorbing sweat and moisture and they extend the life of boxing gloves by protecting them from moisture and odor. They are relatively cheap, and you can find tutorials on how to wrap your hands on YouTube. Buy 4 or 5 pairs.

Boxing Gloves

They protect your hands, knuckles, and wrists from impact injuries. You need gloves if you want to throw a punch; I promise you that bare-knuckle boxing a punching bag will hurt you. Gloves also support proper punching technique and form. Below are some guidelines for getting the right gloves for you:

- 8 oz gloves: Typically used for competition fights, particularly in lighter weight classes (around 147 pounds and below).

- 10 oz gloves: Commonly used for competition fights in weight classes between 147 to 175 pounds.

- 12 oz gloves: Suitable for general training, sparring, or bag work for individuals weighing around 126 to 168 pounds.

- 14 oz gloves: Ideal for training and sparring for individuals weighing approximately 168 to 200 pounds.

- 16 oz gloves: Recommended for heavier individuals or those with larger hands, typically used for training, sparring, or bag work for individuals over 200 pounds.

Boxing Shoes

They make boxing much easier; they are light and significantly improve your grip, therefore your footwork will become better. Plus, it's a given that you need the right footwear for the sport—you don't see football players wearing rock climbing shoes. Boxing shoes help support ankle stability and reduce the risk of injury. They enhance agility and maneuverability in the ring. They allow for quick pivoting and lateral movements. Most of all, they are comfortable and prevent injury. Finally, don't go for cheap ones, think about your feet!

Jump Rope

A great bit of kit for working on your cardiovascular fitness and endurance. It is difficult to get the hang of, but once you do, it works wonders for your boxing ability. Regular jump rope will improve your coordination, timing, and rhythm, agility, and balance. Furthermore, it's a great workout that burns calories while strengthening leg muscles. You can get a jump rope for pretty cheap, so get one!

Mouthguard

This is essential in boxing if you plan to spar or compete. Firstly, it provides protection from the impact of powerful punches, reducing the risk of dental injuries and fractures to the jaw. Secondly, it helps prevent concussions by absorbing and distributing force, thereby reducing the impact on the brain. Finally, wearing a gumshield is often mandatory in boxing competitions to ensure the safety of athletes.

Heavy Bag

There are many types of heavy bags available, and they will provide a great target to practice your punches. While a heavy bag will not hit back, you will get a feel for what it's like to hit something solid and heavy. You can buy bags that hang from a structure or stand up from the floor. They even make bags today that are shaped like an average guy. You just have to put sand or water in the base to make it sturdy.

Speedbag

A light punching bag that is small and filled with air. It is usually hanging from the ceiling or another structure. It moves right away in any direction with the smallest touch. The goal of this bag is to help with speed, rhythm, and hand-eye coordination.

Speedball

This is another tool to help you increase your hand-eye coordination, speed, head movement, and conditioning. The speedballs are inflated with air and usually attached to a wallboard. They can also be freestanding. They swivel when they are punched and bounce back quickly. You must react fast so you can continue to hit your target.

Disclaimer

In this guide I have included a few images alongside the boxing techniques as I believe a visual aid may help with your understanding. Unfortunately, these images seem to have lost their quality when uploaded to the eBook and Print. Therefore, if you would like to view these images to a better size and quality, please download the boxing handbook I mentioned near the start of the guide. In the guide you can find all the images from my boxing guides and access links to videos that may be of great use also. This handbook is completely free, type in the following link to download it:

www.subscribepage.io/boxingtraining.

1.3 Building Your Stance

It starts with a strong foundation. The reason boxing is called the sweet science is that it requires the fighters to be tough, fierce, tactical, and able to anticipate their opponent's next move. The goal is to hit and not get hit, which takes a certain level of brilliance to do so. Those who do not practice boxing in a scientific form will not last long in the squared circle.

Boxers rely on many basic fundamentals as the foundation of their skills and technique. One of the most important aspects is the proper stance. The stance is what makes the boxer. If it's not solid, the fighter will crumble to the ground. It would be like a building with no base, or a chair with flimsy legs.

Your stance is how you position your entire body when boxing. A poor stance makes a poor boxer. A great stance makes a great boxer. The importance of a boxing stance can be summarized by eight crucial attributes that are dependent upon it:

- *The power you generate in your strikes.*
- *Your defensive ability.*

- *Your range.*

- *Balance.*

- *Flexibility with movement.*

- *Security.*

- *Stability.*

- *Mobility.*

Many issues boxers have when throwing punches or practicing defensive maneuvers actually come from a poor stance. Standing in your boxing stance really is not difficult, it may feel slightly unnatural at first but as you spend the majority of boxing sessions in your stance, you will get used to it fairly quickly.

Stance only becomes difficult when it comes to moving around (also known as footwork), throwing punches, and avoiding punches. When you have to focus on multiple things at once, it can become overwhelming for beginners to cope, and that's when mistakes are made. Therefore, spend plenty of time becoming familiar with your stance before cracking on with footwork, punching, or defensive maneuvers.

While there are different types of stances and each one has its variations, there are a few constants that practitioners of the sport need to be aware of. Below I have broken down each body part's role in making a strong stance. I will show you how to position each body part and I will list the common mistakes beginners make in that area.

Feet

Your feet need to be shoulder-width apart. As far as foot placement goes, your lead foot should be pointed forward and your rear foot should be angled 45 degrees to your lead foot. Your lead foot should be planted on the ground, with the majority of the weight on the ball of the foot. For your rear foot, the heel should be slightly lifted so you can improve your mobility. The weight distribution between each foot should be equal. Of course, during various movements, you will have to shift the weight back and forth—but don't worry about this yet.

Being flat-footed in boxing refers to when a boxer's arches collapse, causing the entire sole of the foot to touch the ground. This stance can hinder mobility, stability, and power generation, increasing the risk of injury and compromising overall performance. Flat-footed boxers may struggle to evade punches, generate power, and control distance effectively. A famous example of a boxer becoming too flat-footed—search on YouTube for Evander Holyfield knocking down Mike Tyson in their first fight. You can see that because of Tyson's feet, a simple punch causes him to topple over—the punch wasn't necessarily powerful either.

Legs

You need to bend your knees slightly, creating a slight crouch or squat position. This lowers your center of gravity, making it more difficult for opponents to knock you off balance and facilitating explosive movement. Furthermore, evenly distribute your weight between both of your legs for improved stability and balance.

Putting all your weight on your lead leg is a mistake many beginners make which compromises balance and stability, making you easily pushed around. By not evenly distributing your weight, you reduce your agility, limit your defensive capabilities, decrease power generation in punches and overall, you become pretty sloppy.

Hips

Your hips need to be angled towards the opponent. This provides a narrower target area and allows you to rotate the torso effectively when throwing punches. This alignment also facilitates quick pivoting and lateral movement. Not being at an angle can create many issues, such as:

- Poor Balance: Without the proper angle, your weight distribution might be uneven, leading to a lack of stability.

- Reduced Defense: A squared-up stance leaves your body more exposed to attacks. Your vital areas, such as your chin and ribs, are more vulnerable when squared up.

- Limited Power Generation: When you're not at an angle, it's harder to generate power in your punches.

- Decreased Mobility: Being squared up restricts your ability to move smoothly around the ring. You'll find it more challenging to pivot, sidestep, or circle your opponent.

- More predictable: Without the right angle, you'll struggle to create openings and angles for attacking your opponent effectively. You'll be more predictable in your movements.

Torso

Your torso needs to be angled slightly forward, with the shoulders slightly hunched to protect the chin and vital organs. This defensive posture makes it more challenging for opponents to land clean punches and provides added protection against body shots.

Squaring up shoulders refers to positioning your upper body in a way that both shoulders are aligned parallel to your opponent. In essence, squaring up your shoulders in boxing compromises your defensive ability, reduces your mobility and agility, limits your power generation, and makes your intentions more predictable to your opponent.

Arms and Hands

Always keep your hands up, close to your face, and elbows tucked in. Your fists should be at about eye level, with your knuckles facing forward. This position protects your face and allows for quick defensive maneuvers. Your lead hand should be slightly farther forward than your rear hand. Keep it relaxed but ready to snap out quickly. Keep your rear hand cocked slightly, ready to deliver powerful punches. Keep your elbows close to your body. This protects your ribs and midsection from body shots while also conserving energy.

Not relaxing your arms is an issue that slows response time and reduces flexibility, making your defense and offense less effective. By being tense all the time, you fatigue quickly and telegraph all your punches.

Head

Keep your chin tucked down slightly toward your chest to protect it from incoming punches. Your chin should not be jutting out, as this makes it an easy target for your opponent. Maintain your gaze straight ahead, focusing on your opponent's chest or midsection. This allows you to see your opponent's movements while still being aware of potential punches coming your way.

Many beginners don't tuck their chin and become much more likely to get knocked out. A well-placed punch to the chin can result in a knockout or at least a significant loss of balance and control. With your chin up, your entire face becomes more exposed to punches. Without your chin tucked, it's harder to effectively protect your head and face. Your defensive maneuvers, such as blocking and slipping, may be less effective, leaving you more susceptible to getting hit.

Now, we will cover the two main stances called "Orthodox" and "Southpaw," essentially right-handed versus left. Please acknowledge the mistakes mentioned with each body part, because when you don't have a good stance, you will easily get pushed around the ring like a rag doll. It does not have as much to do with strength as it does with body mechanics. In addition, you get knocked down easily, receive more devastating blows, and cannot hit your opponent back with adequate force.

Finally, I don't recommend copying the professionals. This is because you will create a mirror image, but not understand all the details. A solid boxing stance takes a while to develop. What works for one individual may not work for someone else. You need to find what works for you. Your stance needs to bring out your strengths and hide your weaknesses. If you observe all the great boxers throughout time, they all had their own unique stance that they used based on height, weight, arm length, leg strength, and many other factors.

Orthodox

As we mentioned before, the orthodox stance is for right-handers. For an orthodox technique to work properly, you must stand with your left hand and foot forward. Your weaker side stands out in front, so you can use it to throw jabs and lighter punches. Since your stronger side is towards the back, you can use it for power punches like the right cross.

1. Position feet shoulder-width apart.
2. Distribute weight evenly, with slightly more on the balls of feet.
3. Left foot placed forward and angled outward, right foot parallel.
4. Bend knees slightly for balance and mobility.
5. Have your hands protecting your face, your left hand in front, right hand covering your chin.
6. Keep shoulders and arms relaxed.
7. Maintain focus on the opponent and always keep your chin tucked.

Southpaw

The southpaw stance is the opposite. This is much rarer simply because there are far fewer left-handers in the world. However, it seems to be more common as time goes on with more people being left-handed and boxers training to be southpaws, as it creates confusion for the opponents. Southpaws are often an orthodox fighter's worst nightmare because of how much they throw them off. The opposite foot and hand placements, along with the different movements, can be hard to understand.

1. Place your right foot slightly ahead of your left foot, with your feet shoulder-width apart. Your right foot should be the lead foot, and your weight should be distributed evenly between both feet.

2. Keep your weight centered and balanced between both legs.

3. Have your hands protecting your face, your right hand in front, left hand covering your chin.

4. Keep both elbows close to your body to protect your torso and ribs.

5. Tuck your chin slightly down towards your chest. Your right shoulder can also provide additional protection for your chin.

6. Keep your shoulders relaxed but ready to move.

Actionable Step

You now know which stance suits you best, so it's time for you to practice building your stance. Don't overcomplicate this, it's very simple. Find some open space in your room and get into your boxing stance. Bounce on the balls of your feet and get comfortable in this position. Practice going in and out of your stance and look at yourself in the mirror—does it look right? Do you feel comfortable? Could you get into your stance quickly without losing balance? Do you feel strong in your stance?

If you have to practice this for several days or longer to feel comfortable in this stance, then so be it. It is vital that you create a solid base. A big, beautiful house is nothing without foundation, and your boxing skills are nothing without the right stance.

There aren't many ways to practice your stance because it is a basic position, just aim for as many repetitions of going in and out of your stance as possible. Furthermore, during a boxing session, you spend so long in your stance that it begins to feel natural. As you get into shadowboxing, bag work, and other drills, everything will fall into place.

1.4 Footwork Fundamentals

Boxers are as light on their feet as ballet dancers. At least, that's how it seems. The way many fighters are able to move around the ring while also engaging in a fight with their opponents showcases how good their mobility is. Their great mobility is the result of their refined footwork.

Having proper footwork allows you to get close to your opponent to land punches, and then move out of the way before they counter. Hit and don't get hit; this is the true motto of boxing. Great footwork is what separates the average fighter from the good fighter, and the good fighter from the great fighter. Going back to Muhammad Ali, the reason he was able to move around the ring so well is that he was light on his feet. He understood the concept of footwork down to a science. A modern-day example is Floyd Mayweather Jr. Many people say that Mayweather runs from his opponents. This is definitely a false belief. He actually stands right in front of his opponents but is a defensive master and is able to move out of the way. Yet again, a display of great footwork.

Once you have learned how to create a proper stance, the next step is to learn the art of footwork. I encourage you to practice this concept before learning to throw punches. This will be a great way to set up your offensive and defensive abilities. In this chapter, we will dissect some specific topics related to footwork so that you can become natural as you move around the ring. Unfortunately, the ideas discussed here are not heavily discussed in boxing gyms across the world. Too often, boxers learn to throw punches without learning the importance of using their whole body, including their legs and feet. I do not plan for you to make this mistake.

Before we continue, I want to mention some of the consequences of not paying attention to your feet. Your feet may be just as important to boxing as your hands. The more you work on movement, the more natural and ingrained it will become. Here are some disadvantages that poor footwork guarantees:

- *You will have a harder time hitting your opponent. Your speed and ability to throw a punch are impacted severely by improper foot movement.*

- *It will be difficult to get away from your opponent. This is especially true of a swarming fighter who will eat you alive if you remain flat-footed.*

- *Because of the first two issues, you will become tired much more quickly.*

Always remember that the footwork and movement you use must be somewhat purposeful. This means you shouldn't just move around the ring for the heck of it. Doing this will make you tired by wasting unnecessary energy.

The Methods of Movement

Boxers seem to just slide around the ring effortlessly. Those who put countless hours into practicing their footwork can move swiftly without needing to think about it. Anybody can master footwork, it is simply muscle memory that is achieved by significant repetition which results in efficient movement, impeccable timing, adaptability, confidence, and energy conservation during bouts.

Footwork is the movement and positioning of the feet. In this chapter we cover clear instructions on how to step and move in certain directions. This is important because even just slight errors in movement can cause multiple issues such as poor balance, defensive shortcomings, limited offensive capabilities, reduced mobility, and increased fatigue.

You need to be able to move in any direction with great agility when boxing. Imagine your opponent caught onto your sloppy lateral movement, they would keep you stepping from side to side until you trip over your own feet. Below are all the basic movements covered.

Forward Movement

This is the simplest movement, if your opponent keeps backing away from you as they may have a reach advantage over you or perhaps you want to change your angle of attack, you will want to step forward so they stay in your range of attack. How to step forward properly:

1. When moving in any direction, you must always be in your boxing stance.

2. Determine the direction and distance you want to move forward. Either a small step to close the distance with your opponent or a larger step to change angles or create openings.

3. Begin by lifting your lead foot (left foot for orthodox stance, right foot for southpaw stance) slightly off the ground.

4. Push off slightly with your rear foot, allowing your lead foot to step forward smoothly and decisively. The step should be controlled and purposeful, aiming to cover the desired distance efficiently.

5. As your lead foot lands, ensure that your weight remains centered and your stance remains balanced. Avoid leaning too far forward, as this can compromise

your stability and leave you vulnerable to counterattacks.

6. After stepping forward with your lead foot, bring your rear foot forward to maintain your stance and balance. The rear foot should follow the lead foot, maintaining the same distance between them as before the step.

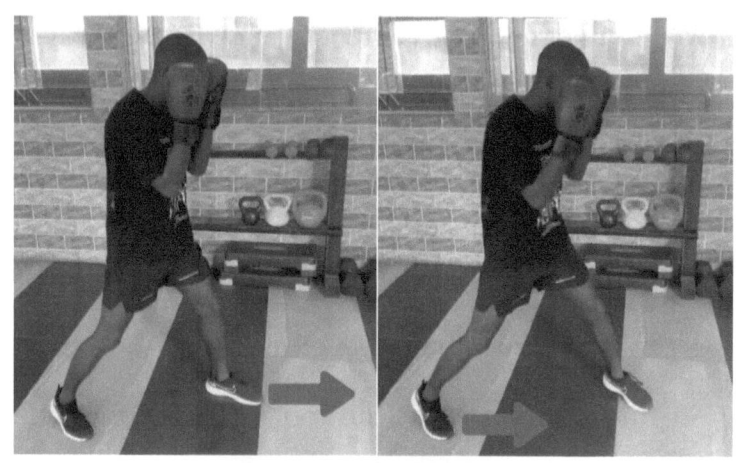

Backward Movement

Stepping backward confidently and effectively in boxing, allows you to control distance, evade attacks, and execute your strategies with precision. I like to be in and out quickly with my attacks, so I utilize the step in and out very often to land my punches and get out of range—of course, the effectiveness of this strategy depends on your opponent. Here are steps on how to move backward:

1. Start in your boxing stance and shift your weight slightly onto your back foot, but keep your knees slightly bent for balance and mobility.

2. Push off with your lead foot and step back with your rear foot. The step should be small and controlled, ensuring that your rear foot lands first. Make sure to push off on the ball of your lead foot.

3. Quickly drag your front foot back to reestablish your stance. Your feet should end up shoulder-width apart again, maintaining the same stance you started with.

4. Maintain a light bounce on the balls of your feet. Always keep your guard up, eyes on your opponent, maintaining awareness of their movements and potential attacks.

5. Ensure that each step back is controlled. Avoid crossing your feet or leaning too far back, as this can make you off-balance and vulnerable to attacks.

The two common mistakes for stepping backward is either when boxers don't push off with the ball of their foot or when they land on their heel. These mistakes cause balance issues, try stepping back onto your heel right now, doesn't it feel awkward? Heel stepping is something we cover in more detail shortly.

Lateral Movement

Moving laterally in boxing allows you to create angles, evade attacks, and outmaneuver your opponent in the ring. Moving laterally means to step to the left or the right. See the instructions below:

1. Begin in your boxing stance.

2. Determine whether you want to move to the left or right.

3. Shift your weight slightly onto the foot in the direction you intend to move. For example, if you're moving to the left, shift your weight onto your left foot.

Throughout the lateral movement, focus on maintaining balance and stability. Keep your knees slightly bent, your torso upright, and your core engaged to stabilize your movements. Ensure that you keep the same distance between your feet before and after the movement.

If moving to the left (orthodox stance example):

1. Push off with your rear foot.

2. Step sideways with your lead foot. The step should be small and controlled.

3. Follow quickly with your rear foot to re-establish your stance.

If moving to the right (orthodox stance example):

1. Push off with your lead foot.

2. Step sideways with your rear foot.

3. Follow quickly with your lead foot to re-establish your stance.

Now I have covered the directional movements, there are a few more that you should be aware of such as pivoting, circling, angling, and shuffling. Pivoting is a fundamental footwork technique used to change angles quickly, avoid incoming attacks, and set up offensive opportunities. It involves rotating on your front while your back foot moves around it. I like to see it as squishing a bug with your lead foot while swinging your rear leg around to follow, which also changes the direction you're facing. The key is to not take your lead foot off the floor. Here's how to pivot to the left and right in an orthodox stance, and alternate sides for southpaw:

Pivoting to the left (Orthodox Stance):

1. Start in your boxing stance

2. Push off with the ball of your right foot to create a rotational force.

3. Turn your body to the left by rotating on the ball of your left foot. Your left foot acts as the pivot point.

4. As you rotate, swing your right foot around behind you in a small arc to follow your body, maintaining your stance width and balance.

5. Your right foot should land in its new position, helping you face the new angle.

6. Ensure you end the pivot in a balanced stance, with your feet still shoulder-width apart. I like to see this as a sharp spin 90 degrees to the left.

Pivoting to the right (Orthodox Stance):

1. Start in your boxing stance

2. Push off with the ball of your right foot to create a rotational force.

3. Turn your body to the right by rotating on the ball of your left foot. Your left foot acts as the pivot point.

4. As you rotate, swing your right foot in a small arc to follow your body, this is slightly harder than the left pivot so here I recommend driving your right knee into the pivot to rotate around smoothly.

5. Your right foot should land in its new position, helping you face the new angle.

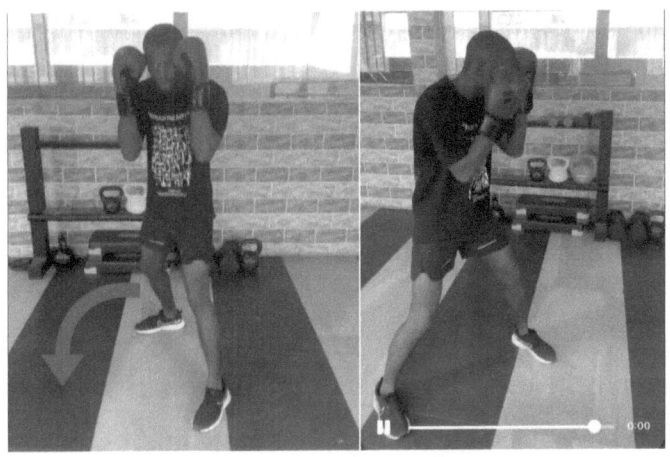

Circling is when you move around to the left or right in a circular pattern to create angles, control distance, and set up offensive and defensive opportunities. I like to see circling as imagining a large circle around the opponent and sticking to its circumference to keep the opponent in a certain position. When you start sparring or fighting, then circling your opponent becomes more challenging as they will be circling you, for now just have the awareness of circling, and perhaps you can practice it by putting a hula hoop on the ground and stepping around it in your boxing stance.

Angling involves positioning yourself at an angle relative to your opponent to create openings for attack while minimizing their ability to counter effectively. Angling isn't exactly a step-by-step instruction you can follow. There are many ways to angle, and to be perfectly honest, the best way you gain an understanding of it is in sparring. For now, just be aware of angling and apply it to your bag work in the future by always stepping around the bag and delivering punches at different angles.

Shuffling involves switching the feet quickly and rhythmically in a short, rapid lateral motion. It's typically used to close distance, evade attacks, or create angles for offense or defense. It can also throw your opponent off. Watch some videos of Muhammad Ali shuffling, he was an expert!

The Body Mechanics of Footwork

Having proper footwork is not exclusive to using your feet. You must pay attention to your whole body. Head-to-toe, it is important to have synchronicity to master the art of footwork. Proper body mechanics are essential. The following are some of the most important aspects to remember.

Keep Your Spine Straight

The purpose of the spine is to support our body by keeping it straight. So, when you are hunched over due to poor posture, you are unknowingly putting your weight off balance. Having a straight spine allows you to be perfectly balanced, making you harder to push around, plus you expend less energy when stepping around the ring.

Your spine is your axis of movement. Whether you want to move or pivot, you will have to make your spine follow your actions. This is something you can try for yourself. Stand with your spine completely straight and then try a few different movements in various directions. Now, try the same movements while slightly tilting forward. Be careful not to fall. You will notice that tilting forward makes the movement more difficult, as it uses up more energy and causes balance issues.

Keep your focus on your spine rather than other body parts. This will allow you to be conscious of keeping your spine straight, despite what movements you make. For example, if you throw a punch with your left hand and keep your attention there, then your natural tendency will be to lean too far in that direction. This will make you more off-balance. If you take a step with your right foot without focusing on your spine, then you will again be off-balance in this direction. Keep your awareness on your spine, inside and outside of the ring. Break any bad habits like slouching around the house, as having poor posture will make boxing much more difficult.

Of course, there will be times when your spine won't be completely straight. For example, when you slip a punch and move in a certain direction, your spine may curve. The important thing is to be upright again as soon as possible. Assess the many great fighters of the past who had great footwork. You will see that they keep their spine straight throughout their fight and move around the ring almost flawlessly.

Relax Your Upper Body

The reason many beginners get tired so quickly in the ring is because of how tense they are. Right now, stand in your boxing stance, and tense your chest, back, and arms. Try to hold it for 60 seconds and notice how uncomfortable you feel. Although beginners won't tense up as hard as you've just done, you can still imagine how quickly you would fatigue from not being relaxed.

True power is generated from the core. These muscles include your abdominal, pelvic muscles, obliques, trapezius, and glutes, among others. They play a major role in your overall movement. Engaging your core allows you to stay grounded as you push or pull. This means any type of powerful movement requires the extension of your core.

How does this all relate? Well, you cannot allow your lower body to feel a certain way without also having your upper body follow suit. This means that your lower body cannot be relaxed if your upper body is stiff. To move properly, you must also keep your upper body relaxed. Punching power doesn't come from being tense, it comes from proper footwork and great timing. I find the easiest way to relax my upper body is to take a deep breath and, on the exhale, let my shoulders sit down as low as possible.

Pay Attention to the Ball of Your Feet

For proper footwork, you must pay close attention to the balls of your feet. With any movement, they must be the first to touch the floor and the first to leave. This means that you must land on the balls of your feet when taking a step and push off with them when lifting your feet from the ground. This will allow you to be lighter on your feet for quicker and more directional movements. It will also keep you from becoming flat-footed.

The worst thing you can do is land and push off with your heels. This will delay your movements and slow you down significantly. You will also have far less balance. You cannot apply force or move in various directions with your heel. Heel walking will make your feet feel like bricks, and you will have no ability to move swiftly.

Standing on the balls of your feet also creates more balance. Try this out as well. Stand with your weight slightly on the balls of your feet and then distribute this weight to your heels. Notice the difference in your steadiness?

The heels have no muscles to work from, and this is why your balance, and power will be off. Even when you are just standing with your feet grounded, you should still have your weight centered on the balls of your feet. You can start practicing walking normally in this manner. You will notice that your lower leg muscles will be targeted too. Just remember this formula:

Toe-stepping = Proper stepping

Heel-stepping = Falling

Create a Narrow Stance

A common misconception is that the wider the stance, the better. There are several reasons why this is wrong. First of all, standing with a narrow stance allows you to take steps and pivot more easily. With a stance that is too wide, you will have less control of your lower body movements because your feet are further from your core.

Wide stances cause you to lose a lot more energy with less range of motion. With boxing, you want to move as effortlessly as possible without becoming too tired. A wide stance will also make it harder for you to stand up straight. More energy will be used to stay upright because the legs will have a certain amount of horizontal force. Your body weight will be distributed to only certain portions of your legs.

Standing with a narrower stance forces you to pay attention to your balance. Many beginners use an excessively wide stance to hide their balance issues, don't. Keeping your feet too wide gives you a false sense of security. Pay attention to the width of your stance, practice going from a wide stance to a narrow stance to build that muscle memory.

1.5 Throwing Punches Properly

This is probably the chapter you were most looking forward to. Punching is the most obvious part of boxing and is the main basis of the sport. If you have decided to skip straight to this chapter, go back and read through this from start to finish. It's good knowing how to punch properly, but if you cannot hold a strong stance or move around the ring properly, then your punches won't do much damage.

There is much more involved in throwing a punch than just shooting your fist across the air and hoping it lands on someone. Just like with other techniques, you need to use your whole body. To throw punches effectively, you must generate power through your legs and core, in addition to your arms.

We will cover many different punches in this chapter and then go into greater detail about the most utilized punches in the sport. Punches come in great variety and can be thrown from so many different angles. It takes a special type of skill and talent to throw the right punch at the right time, while also maintaining your balance and avoiding getting hit. To start, we will list some common punches and describe what they are:

- **Jab**: This is not a power punch. It is usually a lead punch that is used to set up another strike. A jab is thrown straight from the non-dominant arm, which is the left hand for orthodox.

- **Cross**: This punch is thrown from the dominant hand in the rear. It is also a straight punch but generates more power than the jab due to the arm used and the leverage that exists. Also known as a straight punch.

- **Lead Hook**: This is more of a curved punch, and it is thrown from the non-dominant arm facing forward. Very effective at close range.

- **Rear Hook**: This is similar to the lead hook but generates more power as it comes from the dominant arm towards the rear. This is another type of power punch.

- **Lead Uppercut**: This punch comes from below. The key is to bend at the knees slightly and then bring the punch up from below to land on your target. The lead uppercut is thrown from the arm that's positioned in front.

- **Rear Uppercut**: This is like the lead uppercut but is thrown from the dominant arm from the rear, delivering more power.

- **Lead Body Hook**: This is a hook thrown from a slightly lower stance because it's aimed at the body rather than the face or head. It is thrown from the lead arm in front.

- **Rear Body Hook**: Just like the lead body hook, the aim is for a more curving punch that lands on the body. This punch is thrown from the dominant arm in the back.

- **Body Jab**: A regular jab punch thrown to the body. Once again, it is usually used to set up another form of attack.

- **Body Cross**: A regular cross from the dominant arm in the back. The punch is aimed at the midsection.

Once you improve your skill set, you can start including all of these punches in your arsenal. This will make you a more versatile fighter. However, when you first start learning to punch, you are better off focusing on a few punches to become particularly good at throwing them. Some of the highest-level practitioners still rely on a few basic punches. They are just very tactical and measured in how they throw them. You can use the same method.

Punching Techniques

It takes a lot of knowledge and technique to throw a punch that actually has some impact and does not hurt you. Unless you've been properly trained to throw a punch, you are probably doing it wrong. Many people throw punches improperly, so you are definitely not alone. Improper technique usually results in sprained wrists or broken hands, so technique is important for your safety.

I am not advocating violence here. However, if you are throwing a punch, it needs to have the intended effect. To become decent at boxing, you must learn to throw punches properly, no matter what kind they are. To do this, you will need to utilize all the techniques we discussed in the previous chapters. We will break down the steps individually so you can become fully informed on how to punch the right way. You must pay attention to every part of your body.

The first thing to consider is how to make a proper fist. When you make one, your thumb should be on the outside of your fingers and lay at the bottom between your first and second knuckles. In most cases, the thumb will cover the index and middle finger. Don't place your thumb on the inside, you will break your thumb pretty easily. You want your fist to be tight.

Another consideration for your fist is your knuckles. If you are not careful, these can break too. The best practice is to connect your punches using the knuckles of your first two fingers. The punch will be more solid, and you are less likely to get injured. Hitting someone with the knuckle on the pinky finger will most likely cause a bad break, as it is more delicate.

When landing a punch with the first two knuckles, it is imperative to keep the wrist straight as well. Bending the wrist on impact can also cause injuries in this area. Keep your wrist solid and straight as you land your strike.

When you start throwing these punches for the first time, it will feel awkward. You just need to keep practicing and believe me, feeling awkward is better than breaking your wrist, especially if you don't have a girlfriend! You will need to throw thousands of punches for it to begin to feel normal. Just like anything, the best way to improve your punches is with practice—develop that muscle memory so that you can throw an effective punch without needing to even think about the body mechanics behind it. Below are some things I recommend you consider when you start throwing punches.

Don't always aim for the head. The head is a smaller target and most of the time boxers guard their face. Trust me, a body shot hurts and it can knock somebody down, plus you have so much more to aim at.

Don't throw haymakers. A haymaker is essentially a giant wild swing at somebody hoping to knock them out; although it is effective when it lands, it rarely does. Plus, when you miss, which you most likely will, you are left open, ready to take a beating. Also, these punches are so predictable, that as you're winding it up, your opponent will probably have already thought of an effective counter to make you look silly.

Always exhale when landing a punch. You must have heard boxers make a noise each time they punch. They don't do this because they're weird; they are simply exhaling sharply to improve the effectiveness of their strike. Exhaling sharply helps increase power, manage energy effectively, enhance core stability, and is a slight intimidation factor to the opponent—so do it.

Maintain a strong stance. When throwing these basic punches, your stance needs to be strong, as we described before. Also, your hands should stay at the level of your shoulders. As you throw a straight punch and keep your chin tucked in, your shoulder will rise to help block your chin even further. Remember, the lead jab is not a power punch. It is used to set up the rear cross.

Finally, you need to have good follow-through, and I don't mean to shit yourself. Mike Tyson's old trainer used to tell him to throw each punch with bad intentions. This means that the punch should intend to do some damage if landed correctly. When throwing the punch, do not try to land it on the person, but a couple of inches past them. This will make the punch become more effective.

We will now describe the most popular punches in boxing, which are the jab, cross, hook, and uppercut. We briefly covered all of these earlier in the chapter. Our objective in this section is to detail everything about each punch and the best ways to throw them. This will include proper stances, footwork, head movement, and proper defense while throwing a punch.

The Jab

The most basic punch in boxing. It is straightforward and thrown from the lead hand. It is not an overly exciting punch but it has an important job. It keeps the other fighter at bay, helps measure distance, and sets us up to throw more devastating strikes. The jab is known as 1 in combinations.

The jab is a boxer's number one weapon because it lays the framework for how the fight will go. The jab is a long punch that is also quick. It is straightforward and then straight back. It is not likely to leave you vulnerable to an attack because you can get your defense up quickly after throwing it. The jab also uses little energy. The jab is the one punch that can be used offensively and defensively. Yes, it can be used to strike an opponent, but also keep them at bay to prevent their attack. Here are the basic steps on how to throw a proper jab.

1. Get into your stance, but have your lead hand slightly further out than usual for a quicker delivery.

2. To initiate the jab, push off with your lead foot to step forward very slightly.

3. Simultaneously extend your lead hand straight out to punch your target, for the heavy bag aim for the middle.

4. As your arm extends out, rotate your arm right before the punch lands, so the palm section of your hand is facing down. The entire arm, including the shoulder, elbow, wrist, and fist, will rotate.

5. Lift your shoulder slightly just before impact for better reach and to protect your chin more.

6. Tighten your fist right at the moment of impact for a better snap. As your fist tightens, your entire body contracts for explosiveness for a quick second. Your lead foot should also land on the ground at the point of impact.

7. As you land, pivot the ball of your rear foot slightly to generate power and torque in your punch.

8. Once the jab lands, pull your hand straight back to its original position and quickly retract your lead foot back to its original position, returning to your balanced stance.

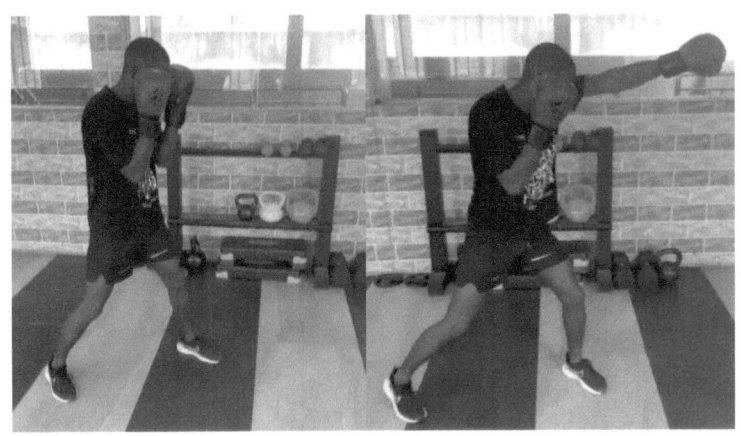

That is the jab broken down into several steps. Remember, it is a quick punch so essentially you will be stepping forward, extending your arm, rotating your arm, lifting your shoulder, and tightening your fist at the same time. The main thing is to not overcomplicate this. Start by practicing slowly and build up speed as you build muscle memory.

You don't need to load up the jab as it isn't a power punch, it is just a simple extension of your arm out and in. The extension should be quick and relaxed. Imagine your hand being like a whip and just shooting forward with little consequence. Avoid tensing up before the punch lands. Otherwise, you are wasting extra energy. Finally, don't telegraph the jab. This means to not make it obvious that you are going to throw a jab, as jabs are quick by following the instructions you will be able to avoid telegraphing the jab easily.

In my opinion, the most common jab mistake is extending the elbow out sideways to look like a chicken wing. The jab must come straight out for maximum speed and effectiveness. Putting your elbow to the side creates many issues:

- It telegraphs the punch. The purpose of the jab is to land it quickly, so nobody sees it coming. If you are extending your elbow out, people will see it coming from a mile away.

- You will have less speed. You are using unnecessary time extending the elbow and then moving into the right position. Once again, your opponent will have time to move out of the way to block it.

- It will decrease your power. While it is not known as a power punch, it should still have a certain snap. Extending your elbow out first reduces the snap effect.

- It is the incorrect technique and will not allow you to use your jab to create openings or force yourself in. It certainly will not keep people away from you.

There are many more mistakes to look out for, but I don't want to bombard you with all the mistakes just yet as it can become overwhelming. Stick to following the instructions and I am sure you won't run into any issues. Below are just a few rules of the jab for further assistance.

Keep your head behind your shoulders. This will allow for maximum defense. If you want to have more reach with your jab, instead of leaning forward, use the step-jab approach. This means to step forward slightly further than usual with your front foot as you throw the jab. This will extend your distance and maintain your balance.

Focus on just moving your arm. There is no need to straighten up your legs, lean into the punch or rotate your foot. The point here is to learn the jab. Remember, the jab is straight, fast, crisp, and surprising. Do your best to make sure your opponent does not see it coming.

So, have a little practice in your own time. Find some space, and just get the hang of throwing a jab to a boxing bag or shadowboxing. Start very slowly, pay attention to the rest of your body, and record yourself. Does it look right? Are you extending your elbow out sideways? Are you lifting your shoulder to protect your chin? Is your jab quick? Is your footwork coordinated with your jab?

The Cross

Most of the time, a cross follows a jab. This is a devastating knockout blow that can put people in a daze if landed properly. The cross is a straight punch that is thrown with the dominant arm in the rear. It is a fast punch but carries much more weight and leverage than a jab.

It is often a great follow-up to the jab because it can be done in quick succession. The best way to describe it is that the jab sets up the bottles, and the cross knocks them all down. The following are the steps for the perfect cross. Of course, based on what your dominant hand is, you can throw either a right or left cross. To keep these steps less confusing, we will cover a right cross. If you are a southpaw, follow these steps from your alternate side:

1. Get into a proper stance with your non-dominant side forward. For this example, it will be your left side. Keep your rear hand next to your chin as you want this punch to travel its full range of motion.

2. Start the punch by rotating your right hip forward while pivoting on your right foot. This means turning your rear knee, hip, and torso in the direction of the punch. For the pivot, the best way I can describe it is to imagine squishing a bug with the ball of your right foot.

3. Shift your weight forward and extend your right arm to punch.

4. As you extend, rotate your arm and hand, so your palm is facing downward.

5. Tighten your fist as you make an impact.

6. After landing the punch, quickly snap back your hand to cover your face.

As you can see, there is a lower body and core involvement with the cross punch. Just like with the jab, you want to keep your defense up. This is why it's important to not leave your hand dangling out there. Bring it back as soon as possible, so you are ready to throw more punches or defend oncoming punches.

The most common mistake made with the cross is looping the punch. The cross needs to go straight out and come straight back. Do not make it looping or circular when extending or retracting the punch. Doing so will reduce the speed, strength, and efficiency of the punch. Your opponent is more likely to predict it as well.

Just like with the jab, you don't want to load up the cross. There is no need to pull your hand back before letting it go to throw the punch. Your arm isn't a slingshot, so throw the straight punch. The punch is powerful enough as it is because you are rotating your body into the punch. Furthermore, you must ensure that when you pivot, your heel stays off the floor.

When throwing the cross, instead of pulling your dominant shoulder forward, you must pull your non-dominant shoulder back. This is known as the anterior/posterior sling. This type of movement is what generates rotational force. Just remember that one side pulls back as the other one moves forward.

Now, take some time to practice. Throw a few crosses when shadowboxing or to a boxing bag, remember to mix it up by throwing to the head and body. Record yourself and review the footage. Ask yourself these questions: Are you pivoting your rear foot correctly? Does your cross feel powerful? Are you quickly bringing your hand back to guard your chin? Are you maintaining great balance and stability?

The Hook

This is another type of power punch that will make quite an impression when it lands. To throw a proper hook, you must be close enough to your opponent to make an impact. Instead of being straight, it is thrown at more of an arc. However, avoid making the arc a big loop. The hook should be short, so it still catches an opponent off guard. It can be used after a jab if you are able to close the distance a little bit. You want to avoid hook punches from a long distance; otherwise, they will not have the same effect. The following are the steps to throwing a proper lead hook, for this example a left hook:

1. Begin in your boxing stance.

2. Load up the hook by twisting your left shoulder and hips back into your lead leg and slightly bring your lead hand off your face.

3. From this position, use your core and hips to release the hook and as you throw the punch towards the target in an arc, ensure you pivot on the ball of your lead foot into the punch.

4. As you rotate, lift your left hand to shoulder level, keeping the elbow bent at a 90-degree angle.

5. Keep your arm at a 90-degree angle throughout the punch. Your elbow should be in line with your fist and shoulder. The hook should travel in a horizontal arc toward the target.

6. At the moment of impact, your palm can face you or downwards, depending on preference and target.

7. After making contact, follow through slightly to ensure the punch has maximum impact, but avoid overextending.

8. Quickly bring your hand back to guard your face to avoid counterpunches.

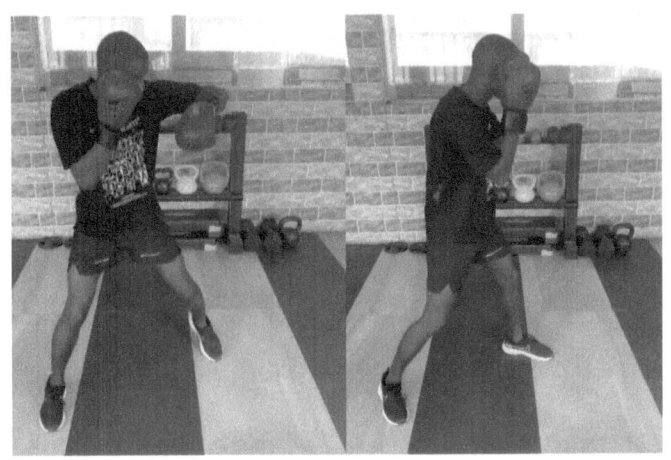

The rear hook has very similar mechanics to the lead hook, it just comes from the opposite side. However, there is no need to load this hook, as twisting your body into it gives you enough power. Below are the instructions:

1. Begin in your boxing stance.

2. Engage your core and take your right hand slightly away from your face.

3. Pivot on your right foot and throw your punch toward the target in an arc.

4. Keep your arm at a 90-degree angle throughout the punch. Your elbow should be in line with your fist and shoulder. At the moment of impact, your palm can face

you or downwards, depending on preference and target.

5. After making contact, follow through slightly to ensure the punch has maximum impact, but avoid overextending.

6. Quickly bring your hand back to guard your face to avoid counterpunches.

We will now cover some basic rules of throwing hooks. First, ensure you wait for an opening before throwing a hook. Hooks are quite easy to defend and counter, so throwing a desperate hook may not benefit you. Punch with your body, twist back slightly to load up the hook, and aim to finish facing

90 degrees in the direction you throw the punch. Pivot your feet and be quick. It is nearly impossible not to telegraph a hook, so throw it quick enough that your opponent cannot react to it in time.

The common hook mistake is not transferring weight correctly. Do not throw this only using the force from your arm. Even though it's short and quick, you must still put your body behind it as you rotate and pivot your feet. Once again, keep your spine straight and use it as an axis for movement. This will help keep your weight centered and your body in full balance.

Since this punch is best used at a short range, having too much distance between you and your opponent is not ideal. First of all, with the pullback, it will be very obvious that the punch is coming. A hook is much harder to see when a fighter is on the inside. Wide looping punches are not highly effective and leave a boxer wide open for an attack. After you close the distance, step into your hook for full impact as it lands.

Just like with any punch, always remember to keep your guard up. As you throw the hook with whichever arm, keep the opposite hand tucked in close and covering your chin. As you rotate, you can guard part of your chin at that time, as well. Remember to keep your hooks tight and close to you so you can bring that arm back to you quickly. Whenever you are not punching, make sure you are playing full defense.

Have a practice, start by throwing both lead hooks to the head and body when shadowboxing or on a bag, I encourage you to use a football (soccer ball) to help you maintain the 90 degrees elbow bend—simply wedge the ball between your chest, biceps, and forearm to create the perfect bend radius. As you progress with your ability, add rear hooks to the mix.

Record yourself throwing hooks and ask yourself these questions: Have you pivoted your feet correctly? Have you followed through enough? Do your hooks feel powerful? Are your hooks quick? Are you using your body well enough to generate the power?

The Uppercut

The uppercut is a powerful punch, and if it lands, it can be devastating. The uppercut is also the most underutilized and improperly thrown punches in the sport. This may be because there are limited pieces of equipment to practice this punch on. Also, this punch, similar to a hook, is meant to be thrown at close range for full effect. For this reason, it is mainly used by fighters who like to get on the inside and close the distance.

The uppercut is a risky move as well because you have to momentarily drop your guard. This opens you up for a quick counter. This is why the punch should only be used when you have a good opening and can throw it quickly at your target. A proper uppercut is short and crisp which makes your opponent's head pop up. With the angle it is thrown from, if it lands on the chin or jaw, it can knock your opponent in a spectacular fashion. Think about the uppercut as transferring energy from the ground up. To throw a good uppercut, use the following steps:

1. Start in your stance.

2. Begin the uppercut by bending your knees, slightly dropping your body down.

3. Keep your hips down and rotate your hips and shoulders toward your lead side - left for orthodox.

4. After rotating your body slightly either to your lead side, slightly drop your lead hand from your face and punch up towards the target, use your legs to drive your body upward. Pivot your feet into the direction of the punch.

5. Keep your elbows bent and close to your body. The punch should travel in a tight arc, not a wide swing (don't over-exaggerate it). Keep your palms facing your body.

6. Transfer your weight from your back foot to your front foot. After the punch lands, pull your hand straight back to your chin. Remember, the punch is just supposed to pop their head up quickly.

When it comes to throwing a rear uppercut, follow the previous instructions for lead uppercut, just on the alternate side. Plus, it may help to be in a closer range to your target.

Throwing an uppercut is fairly complex compared to the rest of the punches explained due to its body mechanics and angling. Take time when practicing this punch, just like the hook, get familiar with the mechanics of a lead uppercut and when you build that muscle memory, start adding rear uppercuts to your game.

The main error that everybody makes is overextending the punch, furthermore, I have seen countless times people jump up into the uppercut like they're some video game character. Don't leave your hand hanging about after landing the punch. It doesn't generate more power and leaves you open for counters. There is no jumping required for any boxing technique, pivoting your feet generates enough power and doesn't make it possible for your opponent to send you flying backward while in mid-air.

Just like the other punches, practice throwing uppercuts to a bag or when shadowboxing. Review it yourself, ask for feedback, watch videos, and get the hang of it. Timing is the most important part of executing a great uppercut, so when you feel comfortable sparring, that is where you get the best practice for this move.

As you can see, throwing a proper punch that will do some damage is not so much about strength, but proper angles and body mechanics. If you look at some of the devastating punchers throughout history, they weren't the biggest and strongest men out there. They just knew how to use their bodies to generate power through their punches. There are certainly fighters who are heavy-handed, and their punches will hurt no matter how they land. George Foreman was one of these heavy-handed fighters. But, for the most, proper technique was key for landing that knockout blow.

When it comes to throwing body shots, you need to use your entire body to drop the direction of your punch. You will come across many different opponents of different sizes, so it is hard to give exact instructions for each type of body shot. Just follow the previous techniques explained and adapt them to reach your target.

I hope this chapter gave you a sense of some of the most common punches used in the sport of boxing. As you watch a boxing match, you probably notice a variety of different strikes being thrown. Many of them are just variations of the punches we have gone over so far in this chapter.

Basic Combinations

A combination is two or more punches used in a specific sequence. In many cases, it is a jab, followed by some sort of power punch. It takes a high level of skill to pull off a combination on an opponent because there is so much to consider, such as positioning, guard, oncoming punches, footwork, and much more. So, for now, we will stick to the basic combinations and discuss how to throw them when shadowboxing or punching a bag.

The key to learning combination punching is to get comfortable with the punches, and also to be able to throw them moving forward, backward, sideways, or moving in circles. With the fast pace that can happen in a boxing match, you never know what angle you may need to throw a punch from. The more practice you have in this realm, the better.

1-2

Jab-Cross. This is the most basic combination in boxing. Many people use the jab and cross combo before they even obtain any boxing skills. The jab is used to catch your opponent off-guard and set up the cross, a knockout blow when executed well. Of course, it may just jolt them a little bit, which is okay too. What I don't recommend is that you build a habit of always throwing a cross after a jab. That would make you an easy, predictable opponent. Furthermore, not every 1-2 needs to be thrown at the head, I can confirm that body shots hurt!

1-2-3

Jab-Cross-Lead Hook. After you throw the jab-cross, you are already in a great position to land a beautiful left hook. You can aim the hook at the jaw or body. Wherever it lands, it can do some major damage. This is where the combinations start to get fun and interesting.

1-3

Jab-Lead Hook. If the jab lands cleanly and disrupts your opponent's guard, it can create an opening for the lead hook to land on the jaw or body. This combo needs to be done quickly and in close proximity to the opponent.

They are the 3 basic combinations I recommend you practice when shadowboxing, punching the bag, or punching pads held by a partner. The final element we will discuss here is the idea of the feint. This is when you fake a punch to throw your opponent off guard. For example, you can fake a jab, and then follow up really quickly with a cross, and then a jab-cross combo. Quick feints are a great way to throw off your opponent. However, they must be done selectively too; otherwise, your rival will catch on. So, ensure that your feints are unpredictable and quick for best results. I like to see feints as throwing the first 10% of a punch, there isn't a set technique for feints, so do what works for you.

1.6 Defending Yourself

"Everyone has a plan until they get punched in the mouth."-Mike Tyson

Floyd Mayweather Jr. is known for winning from his great defensive ability. His exceptional reflexes, elusive footwork, and mastery of defensive techniques like the shoulder roll and high guard made it very difficult to land a punch on him. There is nothing more frustrating than not being able to hit an opponent. You see, each punch throw expends a fair amount of energy and leaves the practitioner slightly open to receive a devastating counterpunch. Mayweather was an expert in this field and used his strategic patience and discipline to maintain his unbeaten record.

The only thing better than hitting is not getting hit. It is crucial to avoid blows in boxing because your offense will become ineffective if your opponent is teeing off on you. Also, it only takes one punch to knock you clean out, whether that's in the ring, down the pub, or walking down the street—you'd much rather not face the humiliation and injury that it comes with.

Some of the most successful boxers in history had the greatest defense. Those that did not have great defense were at least incredibly tough and gritty. Unfortunately, these fighters also had a greater number of injuries and shorter careers. Punches will hurt you when they land properly, and although it is good to condition your body to be able to take a punch, there is a difference between conditioning and getting the shit beaten out of you twice a week.

Therefore, defense is very important. When you are competing against someone in a boxing ring, you must stay alert and never lose focus. Even if everything seems to be going in your favor, never become lackadaisical. Doing this will get you caught, and you can lose the match in a second, even if the rest of the fight is going your way. It does not necessarily have to be the hardest punch in the world; a well-placed punch can knock you down without having too much power behind it.

There is no one-size-fits-all approach when it comes to defense. Each fighter has their own unique style, and this includes how they avoid blows in the ring. For example, Mike Tyson employed the peek-a-boo style where he crouched down low and kept both of his hands glued to his face, only exposing it when he actually threw punches in a surprising manner. He also employed non stop head movement and reflexes. Floyd Mayweather, on the other hand, used the shoulder roll where he could keep his left-hand low with his shoulder forward and his right hand covering his face. The punches that did land usually grazed his left exposed shoulder and did not hit him directly. Other defensive experts like Roy Jones Jr., Bernard Hopkins, and Muhammad Ali all used their own tactics, as well.

It takes months of consistent training to discover what defensive tactics work for you, so first, it's best you become familiar with the basic defensive techniques. These techniques are essential for avoiding punches, conserving energy, and setting up counter-attacks—whether that's in the ring or when walking down the street late at night. We are about to cover the basics of blocking, parrying, slipping, ducking, clinching, and rolling, but before that, let's discuss your first line of defense.

Your First Line of Defense

There are many different aspects to having great defense, such as head movement, hand-eye coordination, understanding the ring, never taking your eye off your opponent, having an awareness of where you are in relation to the ropes, keeping your hands strategically located, and displaying great footwork. Footwork is your first line of defense.

Footwork will allow you to keep your distance and move out of the way quickly to avoid dangerous blows to the head and body. Moving is the easiest way to avoid getting hit. You can basically avoid anything and everything if you just start running. Of course, running makes it difficult to create offense, and since you are enclosed by a ring, you can only run and move so far. The key to effective footwork is to move around the ring strategically to make your opponent miss and become frustrated. Once they become frustrated, it is easy to counterattack. If you move around well and have great cardio, your opponent will fatigue trying to catch you.

Moving around the ring can open up great opportunities for throwing punches at unique angles. You can also avoid getting caught in a dangerous position, like against the corner. If you do get caught in a corner or against the ropes, this is where other boxing techniques will come in handy. Great footwork and movement work especially well against slower, heavy-footed opponents.

Brilliant footwork can also allow you to close the distance. Quick movements can help you get away from an opponent, it is also a great aid for getting you close to your opponent. If you are able to stay on top of your opponent, you can really neutralize their power.

Defensive Footwork Tips

We covered the basics of footwork in Session 1 Chapter 3, but when it comes to using your body for great defense, there are a few more things to consider. First of all, moving around too much can wear you out quickly. This is why it's important to conserve your energy and move in a measured fashion. The more you move around, the more difficult it is to create any offense. If you are not careful, you can lose a fight due to not engaging enough. The judges can score it in your opponent's favor, and in some cases, the referee may stop the fight if you run too much.

It is crucial that when you are sparring or fighting competitively, you don't forget the basics. Great defensive footwork is as simple as staying light on your feet, taking small steps, managing your distance, keeping your head moving, keeping your feet underneath you, not taking your eye off your opponent, and having the endurance to last the length of the bout. It is not complicated, most often poor footwork is a result of fatigue or anxiety.

There are many drills and exercises that help improve your footwork which ultimately improve your defensive ability. The quickest way to improve is by gaining fighting experience. When you feel comfortable, ask your coaches to start sparring because that is truly how you learn to defend yourself. Every opponent you face is different; they will manage to break down your defense in different ways and you'll learn how to deal with people of different sizes, strengths, boxing styles, and so on. Just like anything, experience is the best way to build your ability and confidence.

You need to treat each sparring session as a learning experience, you are going to lose sparring plenty of times. Instead of crying about it, reflect on your performances. Record your sparring sessions, note down where you went wrong, look for patterns, and make an attempt to fix the weak parts of your game. Ask your coaches to help analyze your performance and try to perform better in each fight than your last one.

I understand that sparring might not be an option for you, perhaps you have nobody to train with. First, I recommend shadowboxing with an emphasis on visualization. Imagine an opponent throwing slow punches at you and be sure to use footwork to evade those attacks. Bag work and other drills will certainly help you improve, you'll discover much more about this in Section Two. When it comes to your first line of defense, aim to work on attributes like coordination, reflexes, and agility—this gives you a great advantage in your defensive capability.

There are many defensive maneuvers that can assist your footwork. The defensive techniques will follow later, as they mostly involve dealing with the punch, whereas maneuvers evade the punch. Maneuvers such as angling, cutting off the ring, circling, and switching stances are more advanced movements that I recommend you look into once you feel comfortable with the basics. For now, we will discuss the defensive pivot.

The Defensive Pivot

The defensive pivot allows you to evade punches while simultaneously positioning yourself for a counterattack. When using the pivot, you must keep your front foot planted and use it as a point of rotation. The back foot swings around in a partial circle. This move works well with a bull vs. matador situation; when your opponent rushes in as the aggressor, you will pivot out of the way and use their own momentum against them. As you get out of the way, your opponent will be off-balance which is the perfect opportunity for an attack. If you're quick enough, you could easily get off several punches. Instructions below:

1. Start in your boxing stance.

2. Watch your opponent's movements and anticipate the punch. Defensive pivots are best used to avoid straight punches or hooks to the head.

3. If you're in an orthodox stance, you'll pivot on your left foot. For a southpaw, it's the right foot.

4. Push off your back foot to rotate your body. The pivot should be a smooth, controlled turn, typically 90 degrees, but it can vary depending on the situation.

5. If the punch is coming from your right side, swing your back leg clockwise and your body will rotate to the right, allowing for the incoming punch to miss you completely. Punches coming from your left, do the opposite of above.

6. As you pivot, your lead foot remains in contact with the ground, acting as the axis of rotation. Your rear foot swings around to reposition.

7. Ensure your lead foot turns on the ball of the foot, not the heel, to maintain balance and speed. The defensive pivot is exactly the same as pivoting which we covered in Chapter 1.4. Please look back at the photos there and try to imagine how it can be used to avoid an oncoming punch.

8. Finally, it is likely that after performing the defensive pivot, you are in a great position to deliver a beautiful counterpunch.

When You Can No-Longer Run

There will be times when you cannot avoid a punch—maybe when you're caught in a corner or maybe because your opponent is much better than you. When strikes do land, even if not flush, they do hurt a little bit. If they land often enough, they will wear you down and damage you. If you have noticed any spelling mistakes so far, blame the fact I have taken more punches than the average person.

It is important to have a wide arsenal of defensive techniques because, at some point, one or two of them will fail. You will need something else to rely on. When you can't run, move your head; when you can't move your head, slip; when you can't slip, block. Being able to do all of these things well will make you a defensive master, just like many legends of the past. We will break down each one to give you a better idea of how they work.

Blocking and Guard

Blocking is a great way to defend against strikes without taking yourself out of range. It doesn't require much energy or skill. It is the strategic placement of your hands and arms. Blocking punches successfully involves covering your vulnerable areas such as your head, jawline, neck, ribs, liver, abdomen, and kidneys. Blocking is an effective use of your guard to catch punches.

Here are some pros of blocking:

- It is effective against all types of punches. You can block any punch as long as your hands and arms are in the right location.

- You keep yourself and your vulnerable areas completely closed up.

- It is a safe way to fight at close range.

- It is the easiest way to defend against body punches. It is not as easy to move your body as it is your head and feet.

- Here are some of the cons:

- It is hard to counterattack unless you have great speed.

- You will still take partial damage. Even though the punches are not landing flush, they are still hitting you in some way.

- Does not work well against hard punchers. You won't avoid punches in this case.

- Hands can sometimes block your vision.

- Not recommended for opponents who use a high volume of punches.

- Won't be effective outside of martial arts.

First, let's cover some basic rules of blocking. As you assemble your stance, your arms and hands should be covering your vulnerable areas at all times—this is your guard. When you throw a punch with one hand, you must keep the other hand close to your chin to guard your vulnerable areas. You also need to angle your body in a way that protects you from direct strikes. Furthermore, when throwing a punch you need to lift your shoulder for extra protection against a counterattack. After you throw a punch, you must bring your hand back immediately to keep up your defense.

In boxing, there are multiple areas of your body that can be hit for the opponent to score points on you, and there is a wide variety of punches that your opponent can throw at you, all from different angles. Therefore, moving the position of your guard is crucial to defend yourself best. To block these attacks, you will need to utilize the high guard and the low guard—essentially blocking headshots vs body shots.

High Guard

This is a defensive stance that protects your head and upper body from punches. This is most effective in blocking straight punches. You can also block hooks but it takes some slight readjustment. Here's how to do it:

1. Start in your boxing stance

2. Keep your body slightly angled to minimize the target area.

3. Raise both hands to about eyebrow level. Your fists should be tight, ready to take the impact of a punch.

4. Tuck your elbows close to your body to protect your ribs. Your forearms should be positioned vertically in front of your face, forming a shield.

5. Tuck your chin slightly to protect it and reduce the risk of being hit with an uppercut. Keep your eyes on your opponent at all times.

6. While your hands should be up, don't tense your arms. Staying relaxed helps you react quickly to incoming punches and throw counterpunches.

7. If your opponent throws a punch, adjust your guard by moving your forearms to block the punch. For example,

if they throw a hook to your head, aim to catch the punch with your glove/forearm. If they throw a straight punch to your head, catch their punch with your forearms.

8. Make sure your gloves stay in contact with your face or you will punch yourself in the face when the opponent's fist meets your fist.

9. If the punch lands on you, rotate your head and body in the same direction very slightly to take some of the impact away.

10. The most common mistake is leaning back. The point of blocking is to take the punch with your guard, so leaning back leaves you off balance. There is no need to overcomplicate this, it is simply taking a punch using your gloves as protection. If possible, avoid using this as your main defensive technique because being a human punching bag isn't very good for you.

Low Guard

This is where your hands are positioned lower than normal to protect yourself against body shots. This stance also offers certain advantages, such as improved visibility, increased mobility, and the ability to throw punches from unexpected angles. However, it also exposes your head more, so be aware of this. Here's how to do it:

1. Start in your boxing stance.

2. Keep your body slightly angled to your opponent, with your lead shoulder pointing toward them.

3. Lower both your hands to just under your chin.

4. Tuck your elbows into your body to cover the center of your body.

5. Tuck your chin slightly to protect it.

6. Use your forearms to catch the oncoming punch to your midsection, again be aware that your head is exposed in this position.

7. For body hooks, lean slightly into the side of your body that is taking the punch and aim to catch the punch with your elbow/forearm.

Blocking techniques can be practiced at home. It is okay to train solo at first to get your hand and body positioning right. Visualize an opponent throwing a whole range of punches toward you and practice blocking each punch using the techniques covered. Eventually, you'll need a sparring partner who will throw punches at you. At this point, you will learn how to block strikes, as well as counter quickly with your own punches.

Parrying and Deflection

Parrying in boxing is a defensive technique used to deflect or redirect punches away from the target, reducing their effectiveness and creating openings for counterattacks. Instead of absorbing the full force of the punch, you use your gloves or forearm to guide it off course.

A parry can be used to reduce the power of your opponent's punches. In contrast, a big parry can take them completely off-balance, opening them up for a quick counter and even knockdown. The objective of the parry technique is to use your rival's momentum against them, therefore it requires good timing and anticipation. You need to recognize the type of punch coming and react quickly to deflect it. Just like with other defensive techniques, there are both pros and cons to the parry movement. We will go over the pros first, which are:

- Great for deflecting power punches, straight punches, push punches, and long punches.
- Creates great vulnerability for counter attacks due to the opponent being off balance.
- Useful against shorter fighters to deflect punches as they get inside.
- Great way to make your opponents tired, especially those with a longer reach.
- Of course, there are disadvantages too. Here are some of them:
- Does not work well against quick and light punches.
- Does not work well against curved punches either, like the hook.
- May have difficulty with combination punchers who know how to pull their punches back.
- It can be difficult to do at close range.

- Not very helpful against body shots.

Just like with blocking, there are many different parrying techniques as punches can come from any angle. It is no good trying to parry a cross when the opponent throws a rear hook. We will discuss the down parry, the side parry and the circle parry.

The Down Parry

This parrying technique is most effective against straight punches like jabs or crosses. It is a very simple technique to execute, however, please note this technique isn't very effective against powerful punches; they will just strike your midsection. Here's how to down parry:

1. Start in your boxing guard

2. To down parry a jab, protect your chin with your lead hand and tap the punch down using the palm of your glove.

3. To down parry a cross, protect your chin with your rear hand and parry with your lead hand. Lean back a little while parrying a cross to protect your head if you miss.

4. Remember all you are doing is redirecting their punch, no need to over parry.

5. What gets confusing is if your opponent fights in the opposite stance. The rule is that you never want to have your arms crossed, therefore if their punch is coming from your left side, use your left hand to down parry. Finally, ensure to make this a quick movement, leaving your hands out for too long can cause issues.

The Side Parry

This technique involves your hand tapping the opponent's punch away to the side, the aim is to make the opponent overextend their punch in the direction it's traveling. This can be tricky to pull off on faster punches but is more effective against stronger punches. Here's how to side parry:

1. Start in your boxing stance.

2. To side parry a jab, protect your chin with your lead hand and use your rear hand to push the punch over your left shoulder. Slightly rotate your body into the parry. Keep in mind that quick jabs are difficult to parry.

3. To side parry a cross, use your lead hand to push the punch over your right shoulder.

4. If your opponent is a southpaw, parry their jab over your right shoulder using your left hand and parry their cross over your left shoulder using your right hand.

The Circle Parry

Mainly used for deflecting straight punches to your body and is great at long range. It involves swinging your forearm down in a half-circle to deflect a low punch. It is like a combination of the down parry and side parry, you hook your forearm around their incoming punch to push it down and out to the side of your body. Here's how to circle parry:

1. Start in your boxing stance

2. To circle parry a jab, wrap your rear forearm around their punch and push it to your right side.

3. To circle parry a cross, wrap your lead forearm around their punch and push it to your left side.

I strongly recommend spending a few minutes on YouTube watching examples of parrying as it will aid your understanding of the mechanics. Put them into practice and start on your own with shadowboxing. Imagine an opponent throwing straight punches at your head and body and parry them accordingly. Record yourself, ask yourself: Have you timed the parry right? Are you parrying quickly enough for it to be effective? Is your footwork coordinated with your parrying? Have you set up an effective counter-punch?

Slipping

Slipping is probably the most skillful defensive technique that is out there. You must evade the punch by displacing your head and body to one side, either to your lead or rear side. If done properly, your opponent will be in a vulnerable position, and you will be in the perfect position to counter or escape. Since this is a higher-level skill, it may take a while to get used to it. This is definitely a technique you want to practice with a trainer or a sparring partner. The following are some of the pros of the slipping defense technique:

- If done effectively, you are in a perfect position to counter.

- You will have no contact with the punches.

- It can be done with arms down. This is almost like a matador technique.

- It will break your opponent's punching rhythm when they miss, and you move completely out of the way. Essentially, they no longer have a target to hit. But you must react quickly to get out of harm's way.

Here are some of the cons of slipping.

- If you mess up, you will take a direct shot. A high level of skill is required.

- If you get faked out, you will be in a vulnerable position.

- It does not work well against combination punchers.

- Hard to do against body attacks.

Slipping is most effective against straight punches like the cross and jab, the goal is to slip to the outside of their punch. So sticking to the orthodox vs orthodox stances, you slip towards your left side as they throw a cross, and you slip towards your right side as they throw a jab. Below are instructions for both the lead and rear slip:

1. Begin in your boxing stance.

2. Lead Slip: As your opponent's punch is traveling towards you, pivot on the ball of your rear foot, bend both your knees slightly, and displace your head and torso to your left to just avoid the punch.

3. Rear Slip: As the punch comes towards you, transfer your weight from your lead side to your rear side, pivot on your lead foot, and bend your knees and torso into your rear to avoid the punch.

4. After slipping there is a great opportunity for the counterpunch, depending on the side you slipped to you can deliver a straight punch or hook to your exposed opponent.

5. Don't overslip, this will take you off balance and make you slower. The point of slipping is to be quick, therefore you only need to make your head miss their punch by a short distance.

6. If you are dealing with a southpaw fighter, lead slip their jabs and rear slip their crosses.

Of course, without practice, reading this book would be pointless. First, get the hang of the movement and visualize slipping jabs and crosses. Next, train with a partner slow time and get used to slipping. The key is to be quick and subtle, don't let your opponent know you're about to slip. Furthermore, try not to spend too long on the inside or outside of your opponent's punches as it messes up your balance.

Ducking

Ducking is mainly used for avoiding hooks and straight punches aimed at the head. It involves bending your knees and lowering your upper body to move underneath the opponent's punch. Let's cover the pros and cons.

The pros:

- Ducking is excellent for avoiding hooks, overhand punches, and other high punches.
- Ducking allows you to stay in close range, making it easier to follow up with inside fighting techniques like body shots or uppercuts.

- Ducking requires less energy and movement. It allows you to stay within striking distance without expending too much effort.

- Ducking can disrupt your opponent's rhythm, making it harder for them to land clean.

Now, the cons:

- One of the biggest risks of ducking is exposing yourself to uppercuts.

- When ducking in close quarters, there's a risk of accidentally clashing heads with your opponent.

- Ducking can momentarily take your eyes off your opponent, especially if you duck too low.

- When you duck, you expose your midsection to body punches.

- If you rely on ducking too often, your opponent may start to anticipate it and set traps, like throwing a feint followed by an uppercut or a body shot.

I don't want to kick the arse out of this because I am sure you have ducked many times in your life; I mean it is a basic human reflex. There are just a few things to be aware of when ducking in boxing, instructions are as follows:

1. Begin in your boxing stance.

2. Bend your knees and slightly lower your upper body by dipping at the hips. The motion should come from your legs rather than bending at the waist. This keeps you balanced and ready to move or counter.

3. Maintain a straight back as you duck. Avoid hunching over or leaning too far forward, which can throw you off balance and leave you vulnerable to uppercuts.

4. As you duck, your head should move slightly forward and down, but stay within your own centerline. This minimizes your target area and makes it harder for your opponent to land a punch.

5. This should all be a smooth motion.

The key to successful ducking is great timing, and you can only really work on that with fighting experience. Yet again, practice with a partner and get comfortable ducking all types of punches from different angles. The main thing is to not just rely on ducking as your opponent will catch you out.

Rolling

Rolling, or the shoulder roll is the next step up from the parry technique. Instead of your hands, you use your body to deflect punches. This technique was made famous by Floyd Mayweather Jr., who learned it from his father. What makes this technique effective is that your body can roll off your opponent's punches, while your hands are free to counter at a much faster rate. The following are some of the major pros of the rolling method:

- Highly effective against combinations, unlike the parry.
- Great way to protect the head and body simultaneously.
- Keeps the hands free for quick counterattacks.
- Will deflect the power of the punch, even if it lands.
- It provides odd angles for the opponent and gives an opportunity for tricky punch counters.

The following are some of the cons of the rolling technique:

- Ineffective against weaker punches, like the jab.
- May not work well against counter stances, like an orthodox fighter against a southpaw.

A shoulder roll is proven to be easier and more effective than blocking because it requires less energy and you don't need great reflexes either. The shoulder roll is where you roll your shoulder away from the punch to deflect it away from your head. The punch will then land harmlessly on your shoulder and you may also find yourself in a great position to land a counter punch. Below are instructions on how to shoulder roll:

1. Slightly angle your torso sideways, making your lead shoulder the most forward part of your body.

2. Keep your lead shoulder raised and close to your chin to protect it.

3. As your opponent throws a punch, use your lead shoulder to deflect it. This is done by a small, quick rotation of your torso.

4. To deflect a straight punch from coming from their rear, roll your lead shoulder inward and downward to deflect the punch.

5. To deflect a lead hook, keep your guard high, and when the hook is about to connect, roll your shoulder up and forward to deflect the punch to the outside.

6. Turn your torso away from the punch, moving your shoulder towards the punch while keeping your chin tucked behind it.

7. Rotate your upper body slightly to the side and downwards, allowing the punch to glide off your shoulder.

8. Simultaneously, roll your upper body to absorb and redirect the energy of the punch.

Timing is crucial when performing the shoulder roll. Practice reading your opponent's movements and timing your shoulder roll to coincide with their punches. With practice, you'll develop the ability to anticipate punches and execute the shoulder roll effectively. Yet again, watch clips of Mayweather to see how he does it, he is a master so slow the videos down if you have to as he makes it seem effortless.

Clinching

Clinching in boxing is a defensive and strategic maneuver where a boxer grabs hold of their opponent to neutralize their attacks, disrupt their rhythm, and create a temporary pause in the action. When you see boxers hugging mid-fight, it's not them showing their affection for one another, it is used to manage the pace of the fight and prevent an opponent from landing effective punches.

The pros:

- Disrupts opponent's offense. Clinching is an effective way to neutralize an opponent's attack, especially if they are aggressive or have strong momentum.

- Buys recovery time. Clinching can give you a brief moment to recover if you're hurt, tired, or need to reset your position.

- Negates power punchers. Clinching can be particularly useful against power punchers who rely on generating space to deliver their heavy shots.

- Controls the pace. Clinching can slow down the pace of the fight, especially if your opponent is trying to push a fast tempo.

The cons:

- Vulnerable to inside punches. While clinching, you may be vulnerable to short, inside punches, especially uppercuts and body shots.

- Can be penalized. Excessive clinching can lead to warnings or even point deductions from the referee.

- Loses offensive momentum. Clinching stops your own offensive momentum as well as your opponent's. By clinching too often, you might miss opportunities to land punches or capitalize on openings.

- Can lead to fatigue. Clinching requires physical effort and can lead to fatigue, especially if done repeatedly throughout the fight.

There are a few things to consider before getting into clinching. First, understand that the referee is responsible for controlling the clinch. They will break the clinch if it becomes excessive or if the action stalls. The referee will usually instruct the fighters to "break" and then step back to restart the action.

Excessive holding or clinching without intent to break can result in warnings or penalties from the referee. Additionally, using the clinch to repeatedly tie up the opponent without engaging in meaningful fighting can be penalized.

Clinching involves wrapping your arms around your opponent, you can either do this using the underhook or overhook. Instructions for clinching are as follows:

1. Initiate the clinch—closing the distance by stepping forward or using footwork to get inside their range.

2. Wrap your arms around your opponent's arms or body. Either use the underhook—place your arms underneath your opponent's arms. Or use the overhook—place your arms over your opponent's arms.

3. Keep your body close to your opponent to maintain control and prevent them from generating power in their punches.

4. Keep your head close to your opponent's shoulder or head to make it harder for them to throw effective punches. Avoid leaning your head too far forward to prevent getting caught with a headbutt.

5. Keep your weight centered and balanced to avoid being easily pushed or pulled. Leaning too far forward or backward can disrupt your balance and effectiveness in the clinch.

In the clinch, work on controlling your opponent's arms and positioning. This can help you maneuver them into positions where you can throw short punches or elbows, depending on the rules of the match. As you gain more experience, you discover how to clinch to your strengths and the opponent's weaknesses.

The bottom line is that defensive techniques should never be ignored during your boxing training. It is just as essential as your offense and maybe even more important in some cases. Many professionals were great based on their ability to avoid blows, rather than their ability to throw a punch. As always, the goal is to hit and not get hit.

Section Two: Improve Your Skills

2.1 Improving Your Boxing Ability

2.2 Footwork Exercises

2.3 Punching Drills

2.4 Defensive Drills

2.5 Getting Results

2.1 Improving Your Boxing Ability

"An ounce of practice is worth more than tons of preaching." - Mahatma Gandhi

Now the fundamentals are covered, it's about time we started building on your ability. The only way you can improve your boxing ability is by practicing. See, nobody gets better at something by thinking about it. The reason why the best boxers in the world reach the top level is because they have trained harder than everybody else below them.

Well, that isn't always true. Everybody learns at different speeds, some understand concepts others can't, some aren't able to push themselves as hard as others, some cannot deal with the pressure, some peak early and there are many other factors that determine the level of a boxer's ability.

The biggest factor that determines how good a boxer is, is their technical skill, which is achieved by always practicing using the correct techniques. The first section of this guide isn't for you to read and disregard, for every single boxing session you must punch properly, stick to the body mechanics of footwork, and never take the easy shortcuts in training—that includes only doing 9 pushups instead of 10 in circuits!

By practicing incorrectly, you quickly form bad habits or flawed techniques. This can be particularly problematic for boxing because precision and proper form are crucial for success. Continuously practicing incorrect movements can make it harder to correct those habits later on. You may need to invest additional time and effort in retraining to perform movements correctly, therefore, delaying progress and hindering performance.

Practicing flawed techniques makes you more likely to pick up an injury. Injuries are going to prevent you from training, which is going to dissatisfy you mentally and waste your time. When you aren't training, your performance will plateau or even decline, leading to further frustration and demotivation.

Poor practice can result in wasted time and effort. You may spend hours training without seeing meaningful improvements in your skills or performance. Furthermore, it can erode your confidence. All that training with no progress can possibly cause you to doubt yourself.

Ultimately, practicing incorrectly has a negative impact on your results. So, before you get into these drills, please ensure that you follow the correct techniques. Even if you just plan to box for fitness, although having perfect technique is not completely essential here—it is good practice to follow the correct techniques, and you never know when it may become useful to you.

These drills can be practiced anywhere—at home, at the gym, or you could even spar with the residents at your local care home. I recommend getting started at home since all you need is a bit of open space and the equipment listed with each workout. I have done my best to limit the equipment required for drills, however, when it comes to punching drills, you will need a punching bag. Please ensure you warm up and cool down before and after every workout, and make sure you are wearing suitable clothing—boxing in a dressing gown certainly adds to the challenge.

Timings are difficult to set when I don't know your ability, so please don't feel obliged to stick to them. The timings provided I hope for most beginners to be able to complete, but if you fall short, don't get disheartened, you can always try to complete it for the next attempt. On the other end of the scale, if you are fairly experienced, then I strongly recommend increasing the timing or the intensity in some way. If these drills aren't challenging, then you won't benefit that much from them.

2.2 Footwork Exercises

We have gone over specific techniques for footwork such as how to move, pivot, and the body mechanics. The most efficient way to progress with your footwork is to focus on specific drills that will help you master the movements. Regular training will not be enough, you have to target specific areas in order to improve upon them.

The upcoming drills will help you immensely by making your movements more fluid. Your leg muscles, like the calves, will also become more rhythmic and reactive. This will help you with directional changes while allowing you to start and stop more efficiently. You will be able to move well while punching, which, again, is essential to boxing. As you get better, you will further be able to hit and not get hit. The ability of your footwork can be measured by a few attributes

- agility
- balance
- foot speed
- endurance
- coordination

So these are the attributes you want to work on to improve your footwork. For the drills below, it would be best to start off training lightly and gradually make it harder. You can do this by training more often and completing longer reps. You control your progress. When getting started, these drills may feel difficult and you will probably trip over your feet a few times, don't let this demotivate you, get stuck in!

Footwork Drills

For the drills, I have structured them to be as simple as possible. I start with a brief explanation of the drill, the time it will take, the equipment required, and instructions on how to complete the drill from start to finish.

Drill 1: The Boxing Bounce

This is the most basic footwork drill I could think of, essentially you are bouncing on the balls of your feet in your boxing stance. This is a very light-intensity exercise, mostly aimed at beginners who aren't that comfortable in their boxing stance. You can add small movements in any direction to get used to stepping around.

Time: 12 minutes (3 rounds of 3 minutes with 1 minute rest between rounds)

Equipment: None. Make sure you are in an open space.

1. Start by getting into your stance

2. Slowly start to get a little movement within your stance, transferring your weight back and forth from your lead leg to your rear leg.

3. Once you feel comfortable, rise up on the balls of your feet and add more of a bounce to the movement.

4. Eventually, add a very slight shuffle forward and back. Repeat this for 3 minutes to complete the round. Never stop moving.

5. If you become bored of these small movements, begin stepping forward a couple of steps and take a couple

steps back. Practice your forward and backward movements, make sure to pay attention to what we have talked about in the footwork chapter.

Drill 2: Lateral Movement

This drill helps get you used to moving sideways, as it is common for beginners to cross their feet and trip up when doing this. Yet again this is a low-intensity drill and as you become better with lateral movements, feel free to add forward and backward movements in the mix to become comfortable moving in any direction.

Time: 12 minutes (3 rounds of 3 minutes with 1 minute rest between rounds)

Equipment: None. Make sure you are in an open space.

1. Start in your boxing stance.

2. Step 2 paces laterally to the left, followed by 2 steps laterally to the right to get back into your original position. Keep the steps small to around 2 inches.

3. Make sure each step with both feet is the same distance to prevent balance issues.

4. Repeat this for 3 minutes to complete a round. Don't stop moving.

5. Be sure to increase the difficulty by stepping 5 steps to the left, 5 to the right, always maintain great awareness and start adding forward and backward movements

when you are completely comfortable with lateral movement. You could step 3 paces forward, 2 paces to the left, 5 paces back, and so on—get a real feel for what stepping around a ring would be like.

Drill 3: The Figure of 8

Stepping up the difficulty by adding small obstacles for you to maneuver around, this is still a low-intensity exercise, however, you can easily increase the intensity by completing laps of the figure of 8 quicker. This contains a mix of forward, backward, and lateral movement.

Time: 12 minutes (3 rounds of 3 minutes with 1 minute rest between rounds)

Equipment: Two cones and plenty of open space.

1. Set up two markers or cones several feet apart to create a figure-eight pattern on the ground.

2. Start at one end of the figure-eight pattern in a boxing stance with your feet shoulder-width apart and knees slightly bent.

3. Begin moving through the figure-eight pattern, for the first two rounds only step forward and laterally to navigate your way around the cones. Make sure to maintain the proper body mechanics of footwork, repeat this for 3 minutes to finish the round.

4. For round 3, you should navigate your way round the cones just with backward and lateral movement.

5. As your ability improves, increase the speed and perhaps you could alternate forward and backward movements in the same round when a partner calls out "switch."

Drill 4: Pivot Central

Pivoting is a huge part of boxing, this drill will help you get the hang of pivoting when stepping around the ring and is a fairly low-intensity exercise. This is great for practicing visualization as well.

Time: 12 minutes (3 rounds of 3 minutes with 1 minute rest between rounds)

Equipment: None. Have some open space to practice in.

1. Start in your boxing guard.

2. Take a couple of steps forward, then pivot your feet to the right and rotate your body to follow. Repeat this for 3 minutes to complete round 1.

3. Round 2: Take a couple of steps forward, then pivot your feet to the left to change direction. Repeat for 3 minutes.

4. Round 3: Imagine an opponent in front of you and move in a circular motion around them. Be sure to pivot on the balls of your feet as you move in a circular pattern. Maintain a tight pivot with each step and focus on controlling the movement and maintaining balance as you pivot around the imaginary circle.

Drill 5: Agility Cone Drill

You may have seen this drill used in football as players dribble the ball through the cones. It is also great for practicing boxing footwork, practicing short but quick movements, and maneuvering obstacles to improve your coordination.

Time: 12 minutes (3 rounds of 3 minutes with 1 minute rest between rounds)

Equipment: 5-10 cones. Open space.

1. Set up a series of cones in a straight line, with each cone spaced a few feet apart.

2. Start at one end of the line in your boxing stance.

3. Round 1: Side-step laterally and forward from one cone to the next, focusing on quick, explosive movements and maintaining proper form. Turn around at the end of the cones to get back into it and repeat for 3 minutes.

4. Round 2: Same again but side step laterally and backward through the cones.

5. Round 3: Step laterally and forward past the first cone, then step laterally and backward to the starting cone,

step forward to the second cone, then back again, and continue to repeat this pattern for 3 minutes.

6. As you get the hang of this drill, start focusing on agility, speed, and coordination. Increasing your speed will make it more intense.

Ropes and Ladders

Rope and ladder drills are common agility and footwork exercises used in boxing training to improve speed, coordination, and agility. For rope drills, we are referring to jumping rope or skipping, and for ladder drills, we are referring to plastic ladders laid out on the floor that boxers step in, out, and around. It will all make sense shortly.

Can you remember when you were a kid at school? It was very common for the playground to have hopscotch markings on and plenty of jump ropes around the place. Although schools aren't training kids to be boxers, these games help kids develop a basic level of foot-eye coordination and agility. Therefore, if you have ever played these games as a kid or even today, you will not have great difficulty following these drills.

Rope and ladder drills are the same childhood games but slightly adapted to help a boxer improve his footwork. Jumping rope is a fundamental exercise in boxing training. It helps boxers develop cardiovascular endurance, foot speed, timing, and coordination. Boxers can vary the intensity and complexity of jump rope drills by incorporating different techniques such as single jumps, double unders, high knees, and side-to-side jumps.

Ladder drills are designed to develop agility in boxers. You can practice various movements, including high knees, side shuffles, quick steps, and crossover steps, to enhance agility, speed, and coordination. Agility ladder drills are highly customizable and can be tailored to target specific aspects of footwork and agility.

Both rope and ladder drills are valuable components of boxing training programs. They are easily adapted to fit your level of fitness and boxing ability, the drills covered shortly are set at a low intensity but you can very easily increase the intensity.

Drill 1: Basic Jump Rope

The first drill is a regular jump rope. I strongly recommend building a habit out of this, just 5-10 minutes of jump rope during each boxing session. The intensity at which you jump rope is down to you, when getting started start off light and gradually increase your speed.

Time: 10 minutes (5 rounds of 60 seconds with 60 seconds rest between rounds)

Equipment: Jump rope and some open space.

1. Hold the handles of the jump rope firmly in each hand with your palms facing forward.

2. Stand with your feet together and the rope behind you, allowing it to hang loosely on the ground.

3. Swing the rope overhead and jump over it as it passes beneath your feet. Land softly on the balls of your feet, keeping your knees slightly bent to absorb the impact.

4. Keep the rope swinging and continue jumping with a steady rhythm, focusing on maintaining proper form and timing.

5. Start with a comfortable pace and gradually increase the speed as you become more proficient.

Drill 2: Double Unders

You will find that many boxers have been jumping rope for so long that not only do they make it look effortless, but standard jump rope doesn't really benefit them that much. Therefore boxers adapt it slightly to make it more challenging and this double under drill is a more difficult variation as it requires you to rotate the rope twice per jump. This drill is great for developing speed.

Time: 10 minutes (5 rounds of 60 seconds with 60 seconds rest between rounds)

Equipment: Jump Rope and some open space

1. Begin in the same starting position as the basic jump rope drill.

2. Swing the rope overhead and jump slightly higher than usual, allowing the rope to pass beneath your feet twice in one jump.

3. Use a quick wrist flick to generate enough speed to rotate the rope twice per jump.

4. Land softly on the balls of your feet and immediately spring back up for the next double under.

5. Start with single jumps and gradually progress to double unders as you build confidence and skill.

Drill 3: Quick Feet Drill

Now we are onto some ladder drills. This drill will get you working at a moderate intensity as you need to be quick when stepping through the squares. If you are just getting started, I recommend taking your time on the first few times going through the ladder and increase the speed as you get comfortable.

Time: 12 minutes (3 rounds of 3 minutes with 1 minute rest between rounds)

Equipment: Agility ladder in open space.

1. Stand at one end of the agility ladder in your boxing stance.

2. Quickly move your feet in and out of each ladder square, maintaining a light and rapid pace. You want your lead foot to land in the square first, followed by your rear foot before moving on to the next square.

3. Aim to complete several passes through the ladder, gradually increasing speed and intensity as you become more proficient. Repeat for 3 minutes to complete a round.

4. For round 2, work through the ladder, stepping backward.

5. Round 3: complete a combination of forward and backward steps, switch it up every time you complete the ladder.

Drill 4: Lateral Shuffle Drill

The last drill was for practicing short, precise forward and backward movement, so this drill is for practicing lateral movement. I like to see this drill as zigzagging your way through the ladder. Start slow and increase the speed as you go.

Time: 12 minutes (3 rounds of 3 minutes with 1 minute rest between rounds)

Equipment: Agility ladder in open space.

1. Start by standing to the side of the ladder, with your lead foot closest to the ladder.

2. Step into the first square with your lead foot.

3. Quickly follow with your rear foot into the same square.

4. Step out to the side of the ladder with your lead foot.

5. Step into the next square with your rear foot and continue shuffling laterally through the entire ladder. As you get to the end of the ladder, turn around and go again until the time is up.

6. For round 2, same again, but when you get to the end of the ladder, attempt to shuffle backward.

7. For round 3, shuffle laterally across the first square and go back to start, then shuffle laterally across 2 squares and go back to start. Repeat this sequence for the time given.

2.3 Punching Drills

Boxing punching drills are the cornerstone of any boxer's training regimen, serving as essential exercises for developing speed, power, accuracy, and technique in striking. As we have discussed in previous chapters, throwing a punch requires much more than just extending your arm. It is a great combination of coordination, technique, and awareness of body mechanics.

In this subchapter, we'll explore a variety of punching drills designed to target different aspects of punching mechanics and footwork, providing step-by-step instructions and tips to help you maximize your training results. From shadowboxing to bag work.

Regardless of your level of experience or skill, incorporating punching drills into your training routine can help you sharpen your reflexes, increase your punching power, and enhance your overall performance in the ring. So, lace up your gloves, get ready to sweat, and let's dive into the world of boxing punching drills. Whether you're striving for mastery or simply looking to improve your fitness, these drills will take your boxing game to the next level.

Shadowboxing

Shadowboxing is quite literally fighting an imaginary opponent, therefore it can look very stupid. You probably have seen people do this in public and maybe have questioned the state of their mental health. Shadowboxing is an essential part of training and it is just a simple yet effective way to practice all the boxing techniques. Shadowboxing can be done anywhere. I personally don't do it in public but you are free to do as you like as long as you respect your surroundings.

Shadowboxing is a great regimen to help practice the variety of punches in your arsenal. The concept is very simple; you stand in a space and practice your boxing skills by throwing punches at an imaginary opponent/punching bag. Shadowboxing is a great way to practice proper technique. You can also practice your footwork, head movement, boxing stances, hand placement, and several other defensive techniques. For these drills, we will just focus on throwing punches. Below are a few things to note about shadowboxing.

When shadowboxing, you should never stand still, think of it as a simulated fight. If you are told to shadowbox and your coach sees you dossing around, they may give you a hard time. You can certainly build up a sweat within a few minutes. I recommend practicing in front of a mirror so you can review your technique. Recording yourself also helps you see flaws that you aren't aware of at the moment.

The only issue with shadowboxing is that it provides no resistance. If you plan on never competing, then it's not a problem. It can feel quite boring to punch nothing but thin air all the time, this can demotivate you and turn you into a lazy shadow-boxer. Getting lazy with shadowboxing will do you no favors when it comes to improving your boxing skills. I recommend watching some videos of shadowboxing, because if I were to provide photos, they wouldn't exactly capture the complete method.

Boxers often begin their training sessions with a session of shadowboxing to get blood flowing to their muscles, loosen joints, and prepare mentally for the workout ahead. Shadowboxing serves as a dynamic warm-up that helps boxers get their bodies moving and their minds focused on the training session. Boxers may also use it to cool down after their workout. Shadowboxing at a slower pace at the end of a session allows boxers to reflect on their performance, assess their strengths and weaknesses, and mentally unwind after intense physical exertion.

Overall, shadowboxing is a versatile and essential component of a boxer's training arsenal, serving as a valuable tool for warming up, practicing technique, conditioning the body, developing strategy, enhancing mental focus, and cooling down. Yet again, I recommend forming a small habit of shadowboxing because small changes produce significant results. 5 minutes a day is a great starting point.

Drill 1: Basic Shadowboxing

Boxers shadow box in the way that suits them best, therefore if a boxer's fighting style is much more defensive, then they will throw fewer punches and spend more time practicing defensive techniques. For this drill, aim to work at a moderate intensity.

Time: 12 minutes (3 rounds of 3 minutes with 1 minute rest between rounds)

Equipment: None. Make sure you are in an open space.

1. Stand in your boxing stance and stay light on your feet
2. Imagine an opponent standing in front of you. Visualize their movements, anticipate their attacks, and react accordingly.
3. Focus on maintaining eye contact with your imaginary opponent to simulate a realistic training scenario.
4. Round 1: Begin by throwing a variety of straight punches, jabs, and crosses to the body and head.
5. Round 2: Throw hooks and uppercuts from both sides to the body and head.

6. Round 3: Put it all together and throw a whole variety of punches to the body and head.

Some tips:

- Mix up your punches to keep your shadowboxing dynamic and unpredictable, add feints to practice your unpredictability.

- Focus on technique, speed, and accuracy with each punch, aiming to maintain proper form throughout.

- Make sure you use footwork to move around the space, simulating the movement patterns of a real boxing match.

- Keep your movements light, quick, and controlled, staying on the balls of your feet to maintain agility and mobility.

- Don't worry about using defensive maneuvers at this stage.

- Shadowboxing should be done with a continuous rhythm and flow, moving seamlessly from one punch or combination to the next.

Drill 2: Shadowboxing Combos

This is taking it up a slight notch, each round you will practice throwing a certain combination on the imaginary opponent. This is still a moderately intense workout and helps you develop that muscle memory. Start slow and as you get the hang of the combos increase speed. Also, change up the angles which you punch from.

Time: 12 minutes (3 rounds of 3 minutes with 1 minute rest between rounds)

Equipment: None. Make sure you are in an open space.

1. Begin in your boxing stance and visualize an opponent right in front of you.
2. Round 1: Practice throwing 1-2s (jab-cross) at your opponent, aim for the head and body.
3. Round 2: Practice throwing 1-3s (jab-lead hook) to the head and body.
4. Round 3: Practice throwing 1-2-3s (jab-cross-lead hook) to the head and body.
5. Focus on maintaining proper form, balance, and rhythm throughout the combination, keeping your punches crisp and accurate.

6. Try to keep circling the imaginary opponent, stay at the appropriate distance to land the punches, and maintain a strong guard.

Bag Work

Now it's time to hit the bags, which in my opinion is much more satisfying and practical than shadowboxing as it offers resistance, but make sure to include both in your routine. For these drills, you will be using a heavy bag and a speed bag to practice striking techniques, develop power in your strikes, and improve endurance. It's also a great way to relieve stress.

Safety first, I don't want any of you to break a wrist, so make sure you wear gloves, wrap your hands, and punch properly. I always recommend starting the drills with light punches before putting power into them, as typically those who like to start their session by throwing the most powerful punch possible end up injured. I do also recommend that you at least try out the punching bags for 5-10 minutes before getting into the drills if you have never used them before.

Drill 1: Basic Heavy Bag Drill

A moderately intense drill just to get you familiar with punching the bag. This is the exact same drill as the previous basic shadowboxing drill, just actually landing punches this time.

Time: 12 minutes (3 rounds of 3 minutes with 1 minute rest between rounds)

Equipment: A heavy bag, hand wraps, and boxing gloves.

1. Begin by standing in front of the heavy bag in your boxing stance, with your hands up to protect your face and chin.

2. Round 1: Begin by throwing a variety of straight punches, jabs, and crosses to the body and head.

3. Round 2: Throw hooks and uppercuts from both sides to the body and head.

4. Round 3: Put it all together and throw a whole variety of punches to the body and head.

Some things to consider:

- Don't stand still when punching the bag, keep moving and circling the bag and add feints to practice your unpredictability.

- Don't let the bag swing back into you. Treat the bag as an opponent, also as it is an opponent never take your eyes off the bag.

- This is much more tiring than shadowboxing, feel free to shorten the round or increase the rest period if it suits you.

Drill 2: Combos On the Heavy Bag

Just how we did with shadowboxing, this drill is about practicing the 3 basic combinations on the bag. I have included some additional tasks in the instructions to give you extra variety.

Time: 12 minutes (3 rounds of 3 minutes with 1 minute rest between rounds)

Equipment: A Heavy Bag, Hand Wraps, and Boxing Gloves.

1. Begin by standing in front of the heavy bag in your boxing stance.//
2. Round 1: Practice throwing 1-2s (jab-cross) at the bag, aiming for the head and body.
3. Round 2: Practice throwing 1-3s (jab-lead hook) to the head and body.
4. Round 3: Practice throwing 1-2-3s (jab-cross-lead hook) to the head and body.
5. Yet again don't let the bag fight back, and don't stand still.

Some extras: Have rounds of just throwing body shots, or head shots only, have a singular punch-specific round, throw punches with more power or more speed, perhaps only allow yourself to throw a punch when you half circle the bag, add extra rounds and so on. The possibilities are endless. As long as you throw the punches with proper form and don't half-arse the drills, you will improve.

Drill 3: Basic Double End Speed Bag Drill

This is very different to the heavy bag as it is much lighter and moves very quickly. Therefore, this drill is more suited to help improve speed, rhythm, timing, coordination, and endurance. Follow the instructions below, if you feel stuck be sure to search YouTube for boxers using the double-end bag so you know how to use it.

Time: 12 minutes (3 rounds of 3 minutes with 1 minute rest between rounds)

Equipment: Double-end speedbag, gloves, and hand wraps.

1. Begin by standing in front of the double-end bag in your boxing stance.

2. Round 1: Hit the bag with alternating hands (left-right-left-right). Slowly build up the speed throughout the round. Keep these punches light.

3. Round 2: Throw a jab followed by a cross. Reset by letting the bag come back to the center and repeat for the time given, build up power as you progress.

4. Round 3: Power Shots. Put more power into your straight punches, focus on form and follow through, and ensure you maintain control of the bag.

2.4 Defensive Drills

Boxing defensive drills are exercises designed to improve a boxer's ability to evade, block, or deflect incoming punches while maintaining proper positioning and balance. These drills help boxers develop defensive skills such as head movement, footwork, blocking, clinching, rolling, and parrying. Defensive drills are usually carried out with a partner as it helps to have something to defend against, however, it is still possible to improve your defensive skills alone.

This subchapter offers drills that you can attempt alone or train with a partner to improve attributes such as speed, agility, endurance, timing, reaction time, intelligence, and focus. For those training for a bit of fun or fitness, training alone is great and you will pick up a basic self-defense ability. Furthermore, I have tried to include the whole shebang in these drills, that means you will be training footwork, punching techniques, and defense all in the same drill.

For those looking to get in the ring, I strongly recommend utilizing the 1-on-1 training drills provided as they will give you a great understanding of the body mechanics behind the defensive movements and as you gain experience, you start understanding how to use your opponent's momentum against you to open them up.

Reaction Time Drills

Reaction time drills in boxing aim to improve your ability to quickly respond to stimuli. Examples include visual, auditory, and partner-based drills, peripheral vision exercises, decision-making scenarios, and timing drills. These drills enhance reflexes, decision-making, and situational awareness. Pretty much if your reaction time is poor, no matter how good your defensive techniques are, you won't be able to defend the oncoming attack in time.

Drill 1: Boxing With Cues

In this drill, you are reacting to a stimulus which will be either a partner calling out a certain punch or combination for you to perform or cues from an app you can set up yourself. Whether you do this with shadowboxing or punching a bag is up to you, this will be a low to moderate-intensity workout. However, it requires great focus and speed is the key factor here.

Time: 12 minutes (3 rounds of 3 minutes with 1 minute rest between rounds)

Equipment: Possibly hand wraps, boxing gloves, a heavy bag, and an app randomly shouts cues at you.

1. Start by standing in your boxing stance

2. Have punch combinations or defensive movements called out for you. Examples include: jab, cross, hook, 1-2, 1-2-3, slip straight punch, block body hook, down parry straight punch, and so on.

3. React to your own cues by executing the instructed punches or defensive maneuvers immediately and repeat this for 3 minutes.

What to consider:

- Just because there is a big gap between callouts doesn't mean you can switch off, always stay moving with your guard up and focus on speed.

- I recommend for round 1 to only have cues for punching and combos, round 2 to only have cues for defensive moves, and round 3 to have a mix of all.

Drill 2: Funky Ball Bounce

This is fairly different from most boxing drills, probably something that you would associate with goalkeepers in football. However, it still helps you develop coordination and reaction times. A funky ball is simply an irregularly shaped ball that when dropped could bounce in any direction. This is a very low-intensity workout and can be done alone, but if you have a partner ask them to throw the ball towards you at the ground and you try to catch it.

Time: 5 minutes

Equipment: Funky Ball and open space.

1. Start in your boxing stance.

2. Spend 5 minutes dropping or throwing the funky ball at the ground and attempt to catch it. It may be difficult at the start but as you develop your awareness of how the object travels, your reaction time and coordination will improve to the stage where you can catch it.

3. To make this harder, throw the ball so it bounces off the ground onto a wall, or have a partner throw the ball for you. How hard this drill is also depends on the shape of the ball. I have included a photo below to give you an idea of what they look like.

There are so many more reaction time drills but most of them require some kind of technology or another person to challenge you, perhaps you could find apps on your phone that test your reaction speed and so on. Furthermore, you are guaranteed to improve your reaction time from regular boxing training.

Conditioning

Conditioning refers to the process of training and adapting the body (or mind) to improve performance. For boxing, this includes training to improve cardiovascular fitness, strength, speed, agility, and muscular endurance. As previously mentioned, the average bloke would struggle to box in the ring for 12 rounds of 3 minutes, therefore boxers need to regularly condition themselves to prepare for the challenging condition of a bout.

Conditioning is usually implemented into a boxing session close to the end of the session. Not only does this piss the boxers off who are already fatigued, it pushes them to their limits. Conditioning is meant to be difficult and most of the time boxers don't complete their conditioning exercises because of how tired they are. Coaches don't care about boxers failing, they only care about if they put in 100% effort.

The most common examples of conditioning are circuits that include lots of burpees, pushups, and squats, long-distance running to help a boxer develop mental toughness, or could even be taking body shots to build resistance to attacks. Although this all sounds cruel, it is what makes or breaks a fighter, so if you truly want any success from boxing, you need to condition your body and mind in many different ways to become the best fighter you can be.

I have included 3 drills to condition you in different ways, the main thing is that you put the effort in. In my experience, I have benefited the most from conditioning after completing exercises when I really didn't want to train. You need to put yourself in situations of struggle and test yourself. So, try these workouts first thing in the morning, at the end of a boxing session, or on days where you don't feel like doing anything. Even if you perform poorly during the training, it is better than not giving it a go. Finally, listen to your body, although you want to push yourself, don't push yourself far enough and injure yourself.

Drill 1: Basic Circuit

This drill conditions your whole body using circuit training. You need to evenly train all your muscle groups to be able to perform well in the ring without weaker muscles letting you down. Circuit training is a series of exercises with short periods of rest in between. The instructions below will make it very clear, if you are unsure of any of the exercises included, a quick Google search will sort you out. The exercises should help you develop muscular endurance and strength. Follow the list below in order and you have a great workout, feel free to adapt it to make it suited to your ability.

Time: 15 - 20 minutes

Equipment: None. I recommend a fitness mat and timer.

Rules: Rest for 30 seconds between each exercise, go through the list of exercises twice, and work at a high intensity for each exercise.

1. Squats - 30 seconds
2. Crunches - 30 seconds
3. High Knees - 30 seconds
4. Pushups - 30 seconds

5. Lunges - 30 seconds

6. Jumping Jacks - 30 seconds

7. Plank - 30 seconds

8. Burpees - 30 seconds

Drill 2: Interval Running

Interval training is very similar to circuit training as it contains periods of high-intensity exercise followed by rest. However, interval training is more for cardiovascular exercises like running, swimming, biking, and rowing. For this drill, you will simply repeat short periods of high-intensity running/sprinting followed by low-intensity jogging or walking to recovery. This gets you used to the stop-start nature of boxing and improves your stamina.

Time: 20 minutes.

Equipment: Treadmill or have a running route you are comfortable with, timer will help.

1. Choose a running route or use a treadmill.
2. Sprint for 30 seconds.
3. Walk or jog lightly for either 30, 45, or 60 seconds. The better your fitness ability, the shorter the rest.
4. Repeat the intervals for 20 minutes.
5. Gradually increase the intensity or duration of the intervals as your cardiovascular fitness improves.
6. Feel free to do this with biking, swimming, or rowing.

Drill 3: Core Conditioning

Finally, we have some core conditioning—best of luck. This will be a very difficult and fairly painful workout for those of you who don't regularly train your core/take body shots. This doesn't mean to avoid it, just take it easy on the first few run-throughs and make sure your partner doesn't batter you. You will need a partner for this and some protective gear—I wouldn't worry about abdominal protective gear, just ensure your partner wears gloves and doesn't hit too hard. If you want any kind of boxing success, you will need to be able to take body shots and keep fighting. Trust me, if you ignore core conditioning you will be in for a shock when sparring.

Time: 20 minutes

Equipment: Boxing gloves, hand wraps, optional: body protector.

1. Pair up with a training partner, you are both going to take turns in delivering and taking the body shots. You will also both be completing abdominal exercises at the same time.

2. First 5 minutes: Begin by performing an abdominal exercise for 30 seconds followed by 30 seconds of rest.

Rotate through sit-ups, crunches, leg raises, plank, and Russian twists.

3. 5-10 minutes: Get into your boxing stance and prepare to receive body shots from your partner. Instruct your partner to throw controlled body shots directly at your midsection, focusing on targeting the liver area.

4. Take punches for 30 seconds, take 30 seconds to recover, then throw punches to your partner followed by rest and repeat for 5 minutes.

5. 10-15 minutes: Cycle through the abdominal exercises just like you did in the first 5 minutes.

6. 15-20 minutes: Take punches from your partner again, but your partner needs to throw more punches this time, whoever gets dropped the most has to complete 100 pushups at the end.

Tips: As your partner throws the body shots, relax your abdominal muscles to absorb the impact, slightly turn or rotate your body to distribute the force across a wider area, and exhale sharply upon impact to help dissipate the force and prevent winding.

Defensive Shadowboxing

To be honest, defensive shadowboxing doesn't really exist. Regular shadowboxing should always contain a mixture of punching and defensive techniques, however for the sake of the drills in this guide, defensive shadowboxing is the training method of practicing defensive techniques against visualized attacks. I hope you're still with me...

As you gain experience with practicing boxing techniques, you can begin to throw all attacking and defensive techniques together into the same shadowboxing session to make it more effective and realistic. For now, follow the 3 defensive drills to get the hang of slipping, blocking, rolling, and counter-punching. These shadowboxing drills will help develop your speed, agility, and reaction time and sharpen your technical skills.

Drill 1: Slipping Shadowboxing

Slipping is the action of displacing your head and body to one side to evade the punch. This is done by moving your head to the outside of the oncoming punch. I recommend going back to the subchapter 'Slipping' for a quick refresher as it can be quite difficult to pull off. Visualization is key in this drill, you need to be able to fully picture an opponent throwing straight punches at you in order to slip properly.

Time: 15 minutes (4 rounds of 3 minutes with a 1-minute rest between rounds)

Equipment: Some open space and a strong imagination. I also recommend gloves and hand wraps for a proper simulation.

1. Begin in your boxing stance.

2. Round 1: Visualize an opponent throwing a jab at you every 3-5 seconds and slip to the right to get to the outside of their punch.

3. Round 2: Visualize an opponent throwing a cross at you every 3-5 seconds and slip to the left to get to the outside of their punch.

4. Round 3: Your imaginary opponent is throwing both jabs and crosses at you at random every 5 seconds or so, slip them appropriately and throw a straight punch back to the counter, every 3 or 4 slips.

5. Round 4: Aim to slip straight punches every 2 or 3 seconds and throw a counter punch after each slip.

6. Focus on maintaining balance, staying relaxed, and returning to your stance after each slip.

7. Incorporate footwork and head movement to create angles while slipping.

Drill 2: Blocking Shadowboxing

Time: 15 minutes (4 rounds of 3 minutes with a 1-minute rest between rounds)

Equipment: Some open space and a strong imagination. I also recommend gloves and hand wraps for a proper simulation.

1. Start in your boxing stance with your hands up to protect your face.

2. Round 1: Visualize a range of straight punches and hooks coming to your body every 3 seconds or so, use your forearms and elbows to block the punches.

3. Round 2: Now the straight punches and hooks are coming to your head every 3 seconds, block them appropriately. Pay attention to the difference in positioning your guard for straight punches and hooks.

4. Round 3: Now you need to defend only straight punches to your head and body, make sure you mix it up and attempt to throw some counter punches every 4 or 5 blocks.

5. Round 4: Increase the intensity, think as if your opponent is constantly punching you, every 2 or 3

blocks deliver some counterattacks to the opponent—such as jabs, crosses, and hooks.

6. Ensure to visualize punches coming towards you from different angles.

7. After each block, immediately return to your initial stance position and stay light on your feet. This drill requires a high level of visualization, you may not get it on the first few goes but please stick with it.

Drill 3: Full Defensive Shadowboxing

In this final defensive shadowboxing drill, you will build the habit of practicing all types of defensive techniques and eventually build them into combos with punches also. For all of the round, imagine an opponent throwing a straight punch at you every 3 seconds or so. You will add punches to the last round only.

Time: 15 minutes (4 rounds of 3 minutes with a 1-minute rest between rounds)

Equipment: Some open space and a strong imagination.

1. Get into your boxing stance and visualize an opponent throwing all types of punches at your head and body

2. Round 1: Parrying and Blocking. Cycle between blocking the punches and using the down parry, side parry, and circle parry to deflect the punches.

3. Round 2: Slipping and Ducking. Cycle through the lead slip, to ducking punches, to the rear slip.

4. Round 3: Rolling and Pivoting. Practice shoulder rolling crosses and hooks as well as defensive pivots every now and then also.

5. Round 4: Regular shadowboxing. It is now time for you to add punches and practice all types of defensive maneuvers in your shadowboxing. Be sure to practice every technique covered in this guide and when you get comfortable with shadowboxing, you will shadowbox like this all the time. Try combos like 1-2-slip, down parry-1-3, high guard block-2-3 and so on.

Things to consider:

- Don't neglect defensive maneuvers.
- Maintain great footwork and spatial awareness.
- Keep it even with defending head and body shots.

I understand many of you just want to punch somebody in the face, and shadowboxing can feel quite disappointing because punching the air isn't satisfying. Please stick with it, there is a reason why all the professionals have been shadowboxing every day for many years, it gets better the more you do it and you will begin to notice it pays off when getting into sparring.

Defensive Bag Work

Sorry to have a repetitive theme going on but defensive bag work is just regular bag work with defensive maneuvers and techniques added between punches. A swinging bag can actually hit you back so it's good practice to not let that happen. Furthermore, the double-end bag when punched actually springs back at you with some speed so this is a great way to improve your reaction time and speed.

Drill 1: Heavy Bag Defensive Footwork

The beauty of the heavy bag is that you can move around it and it swings at you, therefore you have an opponent to practice your defensive skills with. For this drill, you will be focusing on your footwork so that you can get in close to land devastating blows and back off at the right time to evade attacks.

Time: 15 minutes (4 rounds of 3 minutes with a 1-minute rest between rounds)

Equipment: Some open space, a heavy bag, gloves, and wraps.

1. Begin in your boxing stance in front of the heavy bag.

2. The heavy bag is your opponent, you don't want it to hit any of your vulnerable areas as it swings back at you, ever.

3. Round 1: Circling the bag. For the first round just keep it simple, circle the bag while throwing a wide range of punches—as it swings towards you just don't let it hit you. You can also practice blocking as the bag swings towards you.

4. Round 2: In and Out. You want to stand out of range from the bag, practice stepping into range, landing a few headshots or body shots (extra points for a combo) then quickly step back out of range before an attack can be landed on you.

5. Round 3: Attack is the best form of defense. Footwork plays a large part in the effectiveness of your punches, so absolutely give it your all to the bag. Throw jabs, crosses, hooks both to the head and body. Most of all, pay attention to your crispy footwork and always stay out of range as the bag comes swinging back.

6. Round 4: Defensive Pivot. Throw a few punches to the bag and immediately pivot to the side as the bag swings towards you to change the angle. See this as a bull vs matador situation. Ensure your body follows the pivot smoothly.

Drill 2: Heavy Bag Defensive Techniques

This drill is for practicing the defensive maneuvers blocking, slipping, and rolling. A greater alternative to shadowboxing as you actually have something to practice on. Again, try not to let the bag smash you in your face.

Time: 15 minutes (4 rounds of 3 minutes with a 1-minute rest between rounds)

Equipment: Some open space, a heavy bag, gloves, and wraps.

1. Stand in front of the heavy bag with your hands up in your boxing stance.

2. Keep the bag swinging so you can perform the appropriate technique on it as it swings towards you. Visualize the bag swinging towards you as incoming straight punches and hooks.

3. Round 1: Body blocking. Only throw body shots to the bag and as it swings back towards you aim to catch it with your elbows, as if blocking a body shot.

4. Round 2: Head blocking. Only throw head shots to the bag and aim to catch the bag with your gloves in a high guard as it swings towards you.

5. Round 3: Head Movement. Although the bag won't swing directly towards your head, as it swings you can still get into the habit of either slipping back to the right or forward to the left; depending on what direction the bag is swinging to you from. Always slip on the outside of the bag.

6. Round 4: Rolling. Throw either a single jab or quick combination of punches and shoulder roll the oncoming punch (bag swinging at you). I recommend looking back to the How to Shoulder Roll section before getting into this.

Drill 3: Double End Bag

A much lighter alternative to the heavy bag that quickly springs back at you after each punch. This drill is much more focused on improving reaction time, head movement and speed. I recommend getting used to the bag before trying this drill. Please follow the 4 rounds as shown.

Time: 15 minutes (4 rounds of 3 minutes with a 1-minute rest between rounds)

Equipment: Some open space, a double-end bag, gloves, and wraps.

1. Begin in front of the double-end bag, in your boxing stance.

2. Round 1: Jab-Slip. To get started simply jab the bag and slip either forward to the left or back to the right depending on how the bag springs back toward you.

3. Round 2: Combo-Block. Throw a basic combo like a 1-2, and as the bag travels towards you block using your guard.

4. Round 3: Speed Punching. For this round, focus on delivering as many straight punches to the bag as possible, don't allow the bag to bounce back at you.

Remember, attack is a form of defense. Focus on speed rather than power. Every now and then, perform a few blocks or slips, this will give you a moment to recover and stay sharp with defensive techniques.

5. Round 4: Freestyle. Throw a wide range of punches and use defensive techniques like blocking, rolling, and slipping. The key is to not let it hit you, especially as you fatigue in this round.

1-On-1 Training

Boxing is a sport that involves 2 people in a ring taking lumps out of each other, therefore the most optimal training method is 1-on-1 training because it offers you personalized attention, improved skill development, an opportunity for quick error correction, confidence building, individualized progression and offers great mental preparation.

The biggest issue with 1-on-1 training is that it can be hard to utilize it. Unless you have a large amount of money and can pay for 1-on-1 training sessions, you will struggle to get enough time training 1-on-1, even at a gym! Although you can easily train with your peers at the gym or people at home, it is likely you lack the experience to pick up small faults in each other's techniques. I know I have just praised 1-on-1 training as the most effective, but that doesn't mean you should neglect other types of training - they all play a crucial role in developing your boxing ability.

Drill 1: Reaction Time Focus Mitts

Reaction time allows for quick recognition and avoidance of punches, enabling effective blocking and minimizing damage. It is fairly simple, the quicker you can detect and react to an attack, the less likely it will put you on the floor. Furthermore, when it comes to delivering effective counterattacks you need great reaction time to recognize the opening and deliver the blow. This drill will work on your reaction time and speed as you need to perform punches on a random cue.

Time: 12 minutes (3 rounds of 3 minutes with a 1-minute rest between rounds)

Equipment: A partner, gloves, handwraps, and focus mitts.

1. Begin in your boxing stance with your partner standing in front of you, wearing focus mitts.

2. Round 1: Flash and Punch. Your partner at random will show a focus mitt for you to punch as quickly as possible. Encourage your partner to switch up how they show the mitts so you can use a wide range of punches at different heights and angles.

3. Round 2: Combo Call Out. Your partner will call out a combination for you to perform on the mitts at random.

4. Round 3: Feint and Reaction. Your partner will flash the mitts at random just like the first round but also throw random feints at you, ideally, you should perform a defensive technique like a slip or block to deal with it.

Drill 2: Attack and Defense Focus Mitts

This drill takes a slightly more advanced approach to the last drill, the focus has slightly shifted away from testing reaction time, although it's still important here, and more towards testing your complete attacking and defensive capabilities.

Time: 12 minutes (3 rounds of 3 minutes with a 1-minute rest between rounds)

Equipment: A partner, gloves, handwraps, and focus mitts.

1. Begin in your boxing stance with your partner standing in front of you, wearing focus mitts.

2. Round 1: Attacking Focus. Your partner will have their mitts showing at all times and it is up to you to deliver as many strikes to the mitts in the time provided. Your partner should constantly be on the move to simulate sparring conditions.

3. Round 2: Counter Focus. Your partner is going to at random throw punches (with his focus mitts) to your head or body and it is your job to evade the attack or use a defensive technique and follow up with a counter punch to their mitts. Your partner needs to ensure they show their mitts after throwing a punch.

4. Round 3: All Out. Your partner should always have their focus mitts showing and they can throw attacks at you at any given notice, it is your job to throw as many punches as possible as well while defending against their attacks.

Drill 3: Parry Sparring

Now we are onto sparring, this drill is a very controlled sparring session as the focus is on parrying. It is very difficult to practice parrying without a partner so be sure to regularly include this drill in your routine. Parrying is using your hand to deflect your opponents punch away from you, look back at the 'Parrying' section if required.

Time: 12 minutes (3 rounds of 3 minutes with a 1-minute rest between rounds)

Equipment: A partner, gloves, handwraps, and protective headgear (optional)

1. Start in your boxing stance facing your partner who is also in their boxing stance; aim to keep it orthodox vs orthodox or southpaw vs southpaw for simplicity. If you can't then suck it up, you can't choose your opponents in the ring.

2. Round 1: Slow Time Parrying. You and your partner are going to take turns throwing a slow straight punch to each other's head or midsection (try to keep it varied). The person not throwing the punch will parry the punch using the parrying technique of their choice. Be

sure to parry their punch to the direction that opens up their body.

3. Round 2: Parry and Counter. Yet again you and your partner will throw punches at each other in turns at a quicker pace and the person parrying the punch needs to throw an appropriate counter.

4. Round 3: High Intensity Parrying. You are no longer taking turns throwing punches, the aim is to actually land your punch on your partner. Be quick and put moderate power into your punches, just don't take it too far and try to knock out your partner.

Drill 4: Progressive Sparring

This is where the fun begins, sparring is a form of practice where two boxers engage in simulated combat. The purpose of sparring is to practice techniques, timing, distance, and strategy in a controlled environment. Follow the structure below, as the rounds progress the difficulty increases, please feel free to alter this drill as your ability improves.

Time: 15 minutes (4 rounds of 3 minutes with a 1-minute rest between rounds)

Equipment: A partner, gloves, handwraps, and protective headgear (optional)

1. Start in your boxing stance facing your partner, if you can get into a ring for this it would be ideal.

2. Round 1: Body Sparring Low Intensity. Keep it light and don't aim for the face. Ensure to utilize a wide range of punches and practice defensive techniques.

3. Round 2: Body Sparring Moderate Intensity. Increase the intensity, put more power into your punches, but head shots are still not allowed.

4. Round 3: Full Sparring Straight Punches Only. Head shots are now allowed, but don't neglect body shots! Only use jabs and crosses.

5. Round 4: Full Sparring. Go for it, just don't get carried away. If somebody gets hurt, stop. The aim of the game is to outbox your partner by landing more punches on them than they land on you.

Drill 5: Pressure Cooker

This drill is designed to throw you off. As a boxer, you need to be able to handle distractions in order to perform to the best of your ability. Throughout the drill, your partner will provide you with tasks to complete while you are training. Make sure you listen closely to avoid punishment.

Time: 15 minutes (4 rounds of 3 minutes with a 1-minute rest between rounds)

Equipment: A partner, gloves, hand wraps, heavy bag, and protective headgear (optional)

1. This drill is a combination of shadowboxing, bag work, and sparring with added constraints to add pressure. It is your job to perform under this pressure, depending on how harsh your partner is will decide the intensity.

2. Round 1: Heavy Bag Reaction. Begin the drill by throwing a wide range of punches on the heavy bag. Your partner will call out a number between 1 and 3 at random as you're punching the bag. 1 is 5 pushups, 2 is 5 crunches and 3 is to circle the heavy bag 5 times.

3. Round 2: Simon Says Shadowboxing. Your partner will call out certain combinations for you to perform, if you

do it when they don't start with "Simon Says" then they must give you a punishment, like bodyweight exercises.

4. Round 3: Unpredictable Sparring. As you spar your partner, they can instruct you to complete any kind of bodyweight exercise and you need to do as they say. They cannot punch you while performing these exercises, the idea is that it will disturb your flow of the sparring.

5. Round 4: Stationary Sparring. You will spar with your partner but you are not allowed to move, therefore ensure you utilize defensive techniques well.

Drill 6: An Aggressive Visit

Nothing will make you panic more than someone constantly coming at you trying everything in their power to beat you. This drill requires you to have a partner who takes up the role of being an aggressive fighter, follow each round to see how you are at a disadvantage and simply need to survive the round. The more you do this drill the better you become at handling intense pressure.

Time: 15 minutes (4 rounds of 3 minutes with a minute rest in between)

Equipment: Gloves and handwraps.

1. Round 1: Backpedal and Lateral Movement. Have an aggressive opponent constantly coming forward, pressuring you. Your job is to move backward while staying defensive. Incorporate slips, rolls, and pivots to defend against punches. You cannot throw a punch back.
    a. Tips: Stay light on your feet, moving just enough to evade punches but not so much that you're unable to counter. Control your breathing to stay calm under pressure.
2. Round 2: Trapping and Escaping. Trap yourself against the ropes or in the corner against a partner. Practice blocking

their initial onslaught of punches, move laterally to escape by pivoting off the ropes or stepping around your opponent to get back to the center of the ring. Each time you escape, trap yourself again and find a new way to escape.

    a. Tips: Don't rush your escape; focus on clean, deliberate movements. Use your legs and angles to get out of tight spots, not just brute force.

3. Round 3: Counterpunch While Moving. Have your opponent constantly chase you around the ring throwing all types of punches. You are only allowed to move laterally or backward. Each time you slip or roll, you must throw a counter in return and return to a defensive position.

    a. Tips: Stay sharp with your counters—don't load up. Use crisp, short punches that are effective but keep you safe.

4. Round 4: Back Against The Ropes. Get yourself stuck against the ropes and you are not allowed to move as you spar with your partner. Use a combination of blocks, slips, and rolls to avoid punches and return punches when you can.

a. Tips: Practice controlling the space around you; don't allow yourself to get trapped for too long. Stay calm while in tight situations.

2.5 Getting Results

"Excellence is not a singular act, but a habit. You are what you repeatedly do." - Shaquille O'Neal

Boxing training is not a one-size-fits-all plan. If you get the opportunity to check out multiple boxing gyms, you will notice that each gym is different from how the coaches structure their sessions. Some gyms host boxercise classes (boxing for fitness), and some gyms split their boxers into groups, normally a group of competing fighters to prepare them for competitions and a group of beginners to help them learn the basics. Therefore, each gym has its own process to help people get their desired results.

Results are the outcomes or achievements that occur as a consequence of actions taken to reach a specific goal or objective. Results often serve as indicators of success or progress toward the desired objective. Examples of positive results include improved technical ability, increased stamina, better body shape, improved resilience, and anything that can be measured.

Processes are the systematic series of actions, steps, or methods undertaken to achieve a particular result. Boxing training is the process that allows boxers to win fights. The reason why I like to use processes and results instead of goal setting is because, after years of goal setting, I realized that it had limited my progress—let me explain.

Goals are great to have as they give your life direction. For example, wanting to get a six-pack is going to encourage you to exercise regularly and maintain a healthy diet. But there is a big issue with goal setting—they aren't great for long-term progress. Goals are mainly driven by motivation. People only take action to get the result, so as soon as the result is achieved, the motivation is lost. Carrying on with the example, people like setting a goal of getting a six-pack for summer, they stick to a calorie deficit and exercising regularly from February to May, getting a six-pack at the end of May, stopping training and forgetting about counting calories, enjoying their summer a bit too much, and losing their six-pack in 3 weeks and lose motivation to get back into training.

The motivation comes and goes because of wanting that certain result. Whereas if you just didn't have a goal in mind and decided to stick to the process, you build great habits of regular exercise and eating well—which means the six-pack stays all year round. In order to win, you need to fall in love with the process. Both winners and losers have the same goals, winners beat losers because they follow better processes.

Habits are crucial for success. We all have habits, some good, some bad. We complete most of our habits without thinking, this is because we have repeated these actions so many times that our brain has developed a system to complete the action effectively—also known as muscle memory. When the brain has a system in place, it doesn't require much cognitive function because no learning is involved. When you make a cup of coffee, you don't even think about the steps involved, you just do it. As you've done it so many times, you unconsciously get a mug, add a measurement of coffee granules, boil the kettle, and make the coffee. The only times you have had to think about it are the first few times as your brain is learning the system for it.

Repeated actions become habits when you can perform them unconsciously, however not all habits are good. For example, if you throw a jab 1000 times and push your elbow out to the side each time, you develop the habit of telegraphing the jab. Bad habits can be undone, it just takes much more time and effort.

Habits form your identity. It is fair to say that if you exercise every day then you are an active person, or if you drink alcohol every day you're an alcoholic. Therefore, if you want to become a good boxer you need to apply small changes to your life that eventually make you identify as one. Small changes such as regular sparring, running 3 times a week, studying the sport every couple of days, and sticking to a healthy diet will eventually result in you being a good boxer. But remember, focus on the process and not the outcome because it can take months or years to become good at boxing - take it a week at a time, aiming to be better than last week.

Here is how I built habits to overcome my social anxiety. Back in the day, I was very socially awkward because of my low self-esteem, so after reaching a very low point in my life, I decided to make a small change to my life—starting a conversation with a stranger every time I went out. Eventually, I did this enough that it became a habit that helped improve my social skills, made me a few friends, and reduced my feelings of anxiety.

I also used to be overweight because I ate a large bar of chocolate most days of the week. I decided to make a small change—cutting the large chocolate bar into quarters and eating just a quarter a day. As I repeated this action, I managed to lose a fair amount of weight as it cut about 300 calories off my daily intake. It's the small changes that compound into great results. I hope that encourages you to spend less time thinking about goals and more time working on processes.

The result you want should dictate how you use boxing training. You aren't going to want to spend hours a week training reaction time drills if you want to get in better shape. You can find information on how to use boxing training for fitness, self-defense, and competition in this chapter. If you just want to use boxing training to build confidence, check out section three.

Boxing for Fitness

Most professional boxers are incredibly fit and have maintained their great shape for years as a result of following their strict training program and diet. I assume that you are either after the high fitness level or near-perfect physique, or perhaps both?

You see, boxing isn't always about trying to punch someone's head off, when boxers prepare for a fight, it is what happens outside of the ring that is most important. Resisting tasty junk food, conditioning early hours of the morning, and going through many other unpleasant experiences are the ugly processes that generate such attractive rewards. So, if you are looking to get in great shape or become extremely fit—best become familiar with a strict healthy diet and regular conditioning.

Conditioning can be any kind of exercise performed for a prolonged period of time, the aim for conditioning in boxing is to continue exercises past the point of exhaustion to develop cardiovascular fitness, muscular endurance, and mental strength.

Diet is a huge factor, you have probably witnessed plenty of people start the gym, and follow a great workout program but struggle to see any gains for months—this is probably because they still live off pot noodles and ready meals. I genuinely believe that there is no point in sticking to a training routine if you aren't going to give your body the correct fuel for the intense exercises. Almost every time I've caved into junk food before a training session, I failed to complete the session and felt quite shit about it.

I know how difficult it is to resist tasty treats; I was a fat kid myself and I still have a sweet tooth to this day—unfortunately; it is just something that I've learned the hard way, you cannot expect positive results with a poor diet. So, before you even start thinking about the results you want from boxing training, make a real attempt to destroy your bad eating habits. The first step to becoming good at anything is to remove the bad, so say goodbye to regular takeaways, or that tub of ice cream when you feel sad. First, get rid of the bad and we can work together on building the good.

Now moving on to the results you want. I have broken down the fitness aspect to boxing into 3 areas below, although it is most certainly possible to get good results with all 3 just from regular boxing training, I recommend you pick one to focus on.

Body Composition - This is how good you look in a mirror. A great body composition for a man is a combination of a broad and muscular upper body, a low body fat percentage, a six-pack, and muscular legs. AJ is a great example of a boxer with fantastic body composition. Getting a six-pack is probably the most popular result people want, and all I have to say about that is that abs are made in the kitchen!

Cardiovascular Endurance - This is the measurement of your stamina. Ways in which you can measure this is with a V02 max test, a bleep test, or other timed cardiovascular exercises. As mentioned, boxers are required to fight at a moderate to high intensity for 12 lots of 3-minute rounds, therefore boxing training will certainly help you get fitter. Conditioning exercises more in particular.

Muscular Endurance and Strength - Muscular endurance is how long your muscles can perform repetitions of certain movements before fatigue kicks in. Muscular strength is how much force you can generate with your muscles. Muscular endurance is usually developed with exercises like rowing or biking whereas strength is developed with high resistance low rep weight training.

So, you now have 3 categories of fitness you can get results for. I encourage you to make your desired result more specific. For example, if you want to look good, what muscles do you want to grow or define? If you want to get fitter, how many seconds do you want to take off your 5k time? If you want to get stronger, how much more would you like to bench, squat, or deadlift? There are hundreds of ways to make your goal more specific, just ensure you can measure the progress. Below I have listed some habits you need to be on top to aid your boxing for fitness journey.

Diet

You need to build healthy eating habits to ensure great progress is made with your fitness. The best way to start is to break bad habits, this includes cutting down on junk food and stopping eating too much or eating too little. You can use some kind of calorie calculator to work out how many calories you should be eating a day. Finally, be mindful of the results you want, if you want to lose weight then aim for a calorie deficit. Here are some habits to build:

- Drink 3 liters of water a day.

- Eat 4 or 5 healthy meals throughout the day—these meals need to make up roughly 20% of your daily recommended calorie intake.

- Take supplements. Do your own research. I like to take creatine, magnesium, multivitamins, and omega-3 tablets daily to boost my performance.

- Each meal needs to be high in protein. Aim for 1.5g of protein per kg of your body weight.

- Allow yourself a weekly cheat meal if you struggle to resist junk food—as long as it's just once a week you will still get great results.

Training

You need to follow a consistent training routine, I recommend that you exercise at least 4 times a week. This in itself is the habit you need to form. For many of you who don't exercise regularly, start small and complete 4 x 30 minutes of light exercise per week and build on it. Get your body used to exercising.

Recovery

Listen to your body, although you may have heard David Goggins say that he never takes a day off, he still gives himself enough time to allow his body to recover from each workout and uses recovery techniques to improve his recovery time. Below are some habits I recommend to aid your recovery:

- 5 minutes of stretching a day. Try to target all muscle groups.//
- Always warm up and cool down before and after training.
- Sleep 7-9 hours a night.
- Cold showers/ice baths after training.
- Electrolyte drinks after workouts to replenish what you have lost.

Progressive Overload

The process of making workouts more difficult over time to allow progress to the results you want. Progressive overload is most commonly associated with weight training but is important in boxing also; here's an example, if you were to start benching 10 reps of 50kg for 3 sets, twice a week for 6 months, in the first month you would notice a great improvement in your muscle mass and strength. As you get stronger, 50kg starts to feel lighter and for the remaining 5 months you would struggle to make any gains as you aren't putting enough tension on the muscle.

Therefore, implementing progressive overload to this benching routine would allow for the muscle to be under enough tension for each bench session to tear and grow back stronger. A few ways to do this include increasing the weight, increasing the reps or increasing the length of reps over the 6 month period. So, build a habit of applying progressive overload to your training routine—I tend to make an adjustment every 2 weeks to my training routine to increase the difficulty.

Keep Track

Tracking is boring and easy to forget, but building a habit of it makes you much more accountable and you can see the progress form in front of you. Track your diet using MyFitnessPal and note down the calories and nutrients of everything you eat and drink, even if you're not proud of it. Track your workouts if you have a fitness watch, aim to track the calories you burn, and rate your sessions in terms of effort. You can track your recovery by making a note of sleep, stretching, and other stuff. I recommend making an Excel spreadsheet of all the things you need to track and work from there, start small and add to it—starting with a long list can be overwhelming.

Finally, life will get in the way. There will be days where you don't perform that well when training or you overeat by 700 calories. Unless you want results extremely fast, these things won't matter too much in the grand scheme of things. It is only when you start building bad habits again when things can go south, for example missing training 3 days in a row or forgetting to track your habits for a week. The longer you leave stuff the harder it gets to return to normal, so please don't feel bad about failing once. The key is to avoid repeating failures.

Boxing for Self-Defense

When you look great in the mirror, it is likely you will feel confident in your day-to-day life. However, confidence easily comes and goes throughout the day, especially when you are being threatened. A stronger sense of confidence is built when you feel able to protect yourself and your loved ones in these situations. Although sticking to healthy habits and getting in great shape certainly helps you perform better in these situations, it is your technical ability and understanding of the sweet science that will get you out of danger.

Self-defense involves techniques, strategies, and skills used to protect oneself from physical harm or danger. It includes both physical methods, such as striking and grappling, and non-physical tactics like situational awareness and conflict resolution. The goal is to ensure personal safety by neutralizing threats and avoiding dangerous situations whenever possible.

There are many ways to develop your self-defense skills. Many people will tell you that other combat sports are superior to boxing for developing your self-defense ability, and they could be right. The main thing is that you become comfortable with your ability to defend yourself, and you can certainly achieve that by practicing boxing techniques.

Regular boxing training will significantly improve your self-defense ability. You will become fit, you will have a strong boxing stance that may intimidate the attacker, you will improve your attributes like speed, reaction time, and strength which all give you an advantage, and finally, you will feel confident.

Sometimes it is funny to watch people pick fights with experienced boxers in the street. These attackers are used to getting a reaction of shock from their normal victims and use it to get what they want from them. However, boxers tend to remain calm and may even laugh at the attacker. Having plenty of fighting experience, boxers are able to anticipate the attacker's movements and intimidate them with their strong stance.

Unfortunately, some attackers carry weapons or attack in groups, so please don't feel the need to stand up to threats when your life is at risk. A large part of self-defense is prevention or de-escalation. The most intelligent move is to always avoid street fights because as extreme as it sounds, one punch can kill. But that doesn't mean you have to give in to them. Boxing helps you build an intimidating aura that is likely to prevent you from being attacked in the first place.

Mike Tyson is a great example of a boxer with an intimidating aura, watch clips of the buildup to his fight against Peter McNeeley. As soon as he entered the ring, he stared down McNeeley without taking his eyes off him once, he was in very good shape and his posture made him seem like the tallest person in the arena. Tyson won the fight before it even started due to his aura, I mean his aggressive fighting style and great technical ability also played a large part, but you see what I mean. Anybody can build an intimidating aura, follow the tips below:

- **Maintain a strong posture**: Stand up tall, keep your shoulders pulled back, and take up as much space as possible. Walk around with confidence, and act like you own the place.

- **Maintain eye contact**: Never take your eye off the opponent, aim to make them look away before you do and when they look away keep staring at them. Let them know you are in control.

- **Take deep breaths and stay calm**: Take control of the situation. Show your opponent you are not scared.

- **Remember your training**: Think about all the hours you have put into building your boxing ability and body to become who you are today. You have most likely outworked your opponent and this gives you the upper hand.

Finally, there is no need to beat your chest like an ape or start screaming - you will just look like a strange bloke. It is all about finding what works for you, I am sure it is highly unlikely you run into any danger on the street, just ensure you don't walk down dodgy alleys, don't get blackout drunk on your own, and don't be the one starting fights.

Improving Your Self-Defense Ability

The best way to improve your self-defense ability is by gaining fighting experience; you benefit so much from regular sparring at the gym. By sparring a wide range of opponents, you expose yourself to different types of attacks. You learn how to manage different fighting styles and learn how to deal with fighters of different sizes. You need this exposure to new fighting experiences to develop strategies that aid your performance.

Trust your instincts. Your gut feeling is usually right—without getting too biological, the human body has various processes that deal with perceived threats in the most effective way. So, when you are in danger and you feel the instinct to act a certain way, it is probably best you act that way. You will get a great rush of adrenaline from "fight-or-flight" . It is up to you to benefit from that enhancement.

Target their weaknesses. Everybody has a weakness, although it may be challenging to find it in the heat of the moment, look for any injuries, lack of fitness, or mobility issues and try to exploit them. Furthermore, you can attempt to distract them to get away.

Practice realistic scenarios. You and a few friends can put yourself in scenarios where you get attacked and you go through multiple ways of defending yourself. Have scenarios where you are cornered, or with a loved one who cannot defend themself. This will lessen the shock you get on your first experience when self-defense is required, you will have a rough idea of how to get out of danger and as they all say, practice makes perfect.

When it comes to building habits to improve your self-defense ability, don't pick fights with people on the street. The best habit you can stick to that would ensure future success with self-defense is to regularly complete boxing training. Work on building a strong stance, building your body, maintaining a great level of fitness, building strong relationships with others at the gym, and enjoying it.

Boxing for Competition

If you plan to compete in the ring, you have a long way to go. You have plenty of suffering coming your way, but don't panic, this suffering will shape you into a better person. This is when boxing will become your life—you need to give boxing 110% if you want to step in the ring. It is relentless in the boxing world, people will do anything to beat you and the only person who can prevent that is you. In this subchapter, you will find many tips to up your game.

Study Boxing

There are hundreds if not thousands of articles, books, videos, fights, and other resources that you can use to increase your knowledge of the sport.

When getting started, get into the habit of watching instructional videos and tutorials featuring professional boxers, coaches, and trainers. YouTube offers many instructional videos that explore technique, strategy, training drills, and conditioning exercises. Sometimes, watching videos of certain techniques can help you understand the science behind them.

As you progress, watch boxing matches featuring top-level fighters to study their techniques, tactics, and strategies. Pay attention to how they move, position themselves, set up punches, and defend against attacks. Analyze their footwork, timing, and ring awareness.

When training, it is important you seek feedback and guidance from experienced coaches, trainers, and sparring partners to identify any areas that need improvement and to fine-tune your skills. Be open to constructive criticism and actively work on addressing weaknesses. People can see the errors you can't most of the time, so swallow your pride and let them help you.

Take Advantage of Online Communities

On Facebook or Reddit, you can find many boxing groups dedicated to training. You can chat with other experienced boxers, discover how to avoid common mistakes, and have the support of others.

Everybody Learns Differently

If that means after a boxing session you need to sit down and write about everything you have just learned, then definitely do so. Treat boxing like you are studying for an exam at school, turning up to a session is just half the job done.

Join a Boxing Gym

You can learn the boxing basics and practice your skills by taking action on the information provided in this book, but it's not going to be enough to allow you to win a fight. You need to be training regularly at a gym to have multiple sparring opponents, attention from coaches, access to all types of equipment and a team behind you that wants you to succeed. This motivation from the gym makes it hard to fail. If you like, use this guide to build up a basic ability so you feel confident joining a gym.

Work Closely with Coaches

Coaches have years of experience, they can see things you can't. They always do what's best for you, even if you think they are being harsh by making you run that extra mile. They are pushing you to be the best version of yourself.

Push Yourself

If you want it that badly then there are no excuses for missing a training session or eating a chocolate bar. You know what you have to do, be the voice in the back of your head that says no to temptation. Make a habit of doing something difficult every day when you don't feel like it.

Gain Experience

So many people overlook this, boxers spend so much time looking for ways to become better boxers instead of actually training. Training is what will make you better, the more you train the better you become. It is that simple, work, work, work.

Go all in. You don't know what you are truly capable of unless you try your very best. Picture yourself, a 70-year-old having never stepped into the ring. The only thought that runs through your head every single day—why didn't I try my absolute best?

- I would like to end this section with a few questions to help you think about what you truly want from boxing or life in general.
- What is actually stopping you from trying your very best?
- Does boxing help you feel more in control of your emotions?
- Do you feel more confident in day-to-day life knowing you are able to keep yourself safe?
- What is the hardest part of boxing, and how have you managed to overcome it?
- Has your boxing journey gotten easier as you have progressed?
- Would you rather let your achievements speak for themself, or talk about what you are going to do and never live up to it?

- How many times have you told yourself you are going to do something and have not done it?

- If you could go back in time to 5 years ago, what would you do differently and are you applying these rules to your life today?

Section Three: Build Confidence

3.1 Self Awareness

3.2 Changing Your Identity

3.3 Understanding Confidence

3.4 Pushing Your Limits

3.5 Overcoming Setbacks

3.6 Strength in Numbers

3.7 Champions Mentality

A Chump Named Jay

A few months after Alex joined my gym, another chump strolled in for his first session, his name was Jay. While he made his intentions clear to me in the sense that he wanted to change his ways and start working toward improving his fitness levels, he showed little indication of actually doing so.

For starters, he showed up late for training on multiple occasions, and by the time he changed into his gear and laced up his boots, and pitched up on the gym floor, he *still* lacked the enthusiasm that usually gets me excited. Lacking motivation, he never followed instructions that well, and even any indication of him going through the motions was half-hearted at best.

He clearly lacked discipline, and not only did he insist on continuing to eat junk food, he regularly drank and smoked too. If I was to make any progress with this chump, I had my work cut out for me. He had his work cut out too; if he was interested.

I was intrigued to learn from a leadership coach who suggested that no one is inherently weak and that if we perceive ourselves to be weak, it's only because we are lacking in self-awareness. That said, when we are self-aware, we're able to make better decisions, communicate effectively, and be confident both inside and outside the boxing ring.

Whether you still need to master the basics of boxing in the gym or are drilling yourself with the skills you've acquired, trust me when I say that you'll get better with time. With an emphasis placed on building your confidence levels, getting better in the ring becomes possible. Anyway, let's cover many principles which help build and maintain confidence, inside and outside of the ring.

3.1 Self-Awareness

The ability to become more self-aware of your capabilities, as well as your surroundings, is a stepping stone toward building confidence. I may as well add that becoming acutely aware of your opponent's next move in the ring will help as well. But it's your self-awareness, as well as your confidence, that allows you to meet, match, counter, and defeat every action delivered by your opponent.

Once you've learned how to develop self-awareness, you'll still need to make regular assessments of your abilities inside and outside the ring a habit. Treat this as a routine exercise, just as you would the development and practice of your boxing skills.

If you're self-aware, you're not only aware of who you are as an individual but of your personality as well. You're even aware of your strengths and weaknesses.

Psychologists, on the other hand, define self-awareness as an ability to focus on the self. If you're able to do that, you're able to interpret and assess your actions, thoughts, and/or emotions. A highly developed sense of self-awareness also helps you to correctly understand how others, including your rivals in the ring, perceive you.

How to Develop Self-Awareness

An effective strategy toward creating the best version of yourself is a technique we have already discussed: visualization. You can use visualization to ask yourself questions about your skills, abilities, and—most importantly—your achievements. So, if you've not met the expectations you set for yourself at an earlier time, you'll be in a position to address these once you've mastered the ability to picture how you see yourself developing in the future. Other exercises I favor in helping to develop greater self-awareness include the following:

- **Regular journaling**: Through regular journaling, you'll recognize patterns that aren't working for you. Not to worry if you do because you'll be able to address these. By asking yourself questions such as how you were feeling and what challenges you faced, you'll also be able to make further improvements in those patterns that have been working well for you.

- **Practicing mindfulness**: One mindfulness exercise you should be doing before and after you start training is a deep breathing exercise. Doing this exercise will also serve you well when you're preparing yourself for a fight. Outside of fighting in the ring, you'll be doing less stressful exercises such as meditation, and focused walking. Walking can be included on your so-called off days when you won't be doing a five-mile run. Mindfulness is great because it also helps to prevent you from overtraining.

- **Exercising your brain:** You can do this exercise well by first assessing your own performance levels, and how you can improve on this in the future. This is also a good time to visualize how you see yourself in the future. While you need to be aware of them, don't pay too much attention to setbacks at this stage because we'll be addressing setbacks later on in the chapter.

Before taking a deeper dive into the many methods to develop self awareness, I would like to share a method that worked for me. Running without music. I used to hate running, so listening to music was the little bit of motivation that helped me stick to it, however the day my earphones were broken and I was due a run, it gave me a great sense of self awareness. I really recommend you try it, there is something about being alone with your thoughts during intense physical exertion that gives you complete mental clarity. I now see this as therapy, hope you can too.

Reflection

A great source of reflection is the journaling exercise I introduced to you earlier. During this writing exercise (which doesn't need to last longer than 10 minutes every other day), you'll note down all the things that are on your mind. You'll also use this reflection opportunity to set new objectives for yourself. Writing about how you're feeling will also help you to improve your ability to be self-aware.

What also helps is being thankful for all that you have going for you. During this time, you're allowed to celebrate your achievements, all within reason of course, not forgetting that you still need to maintain your discipline for training.

Seeking Feedback

True to form, your coach is your best bet for feedback when you're seeking to assess your performance in the ring. But who do you turn to in other areas of your life? After all, your ability to adapt well to your surroundings is a crucial aspect of doing well in a sport that demands a lot from you.

Whether it's your wife or parents at home, colleagues at work, or most especially, your coach and training partners down at the gym, it's imperative that you call on the advice of people you trust. It's also useful for you to have the ear of people with different perspectives.

Whether they're from anonymous sources or people you know, the feedback you receive needs to be objective, and while nothing is taken for granted, any negative criticism you receive should never be taken personally. It will help you to improve where necessary and you will also be given credit where it's due.

Assessing Your Surroundings and Environment

This type of assessment might initially be challenging for a chump who's living in a rough neighborhood. But the challenge of changing your environment for the better is well worth it if it's going to help improve your performance. This may entail leaving your gym for a better-equipped environment that welcomes all comers without prejudice.

A greater sense of self-awareness will help you make a good judgment call if you need to change your operating environment. You're able to trust your gut. At the same time, you still need to take note of the kind of people you're surrounded with. They should never be a bad influence on you, and while you need to stay fully focused on what you want to achieve, you need to work toward minimizing distractions as far as possible.

You also need to plan for the worst. This is not a negative piece of advice. Rather, it's an opportunity to be better prepared to make changes at short notice, if necessary.

Addressing Your Strengths and Weaknesses

By the time you're able to set objectives for yourself, note that you'll still need to assess them. You have a better chance of getting results if they're realistic. If your confidence levels have improved, you'll also be more self-aware, and better equipped to give yourself regular assessments, not forgetting that you can still ask others for their opinion. Remember too that you'll be better able to take constructive criticism on the chin, just as a champion would. The easiest way to do this is to write down your strengths and weaknesses on paper and come back to it regularly, seeing if you are able to move certain areas of your game from weakness to strength.

Setting Boundaries

After all the challenges you've faced up to now, why would you want to create more problems for yourself by taking on even more, so much more that you couldn't possibly manage?

You don't need to because you can set boundaries for yourself, and by doing so, you won't be losing your sense of self. You won't be losing your identity either. Rather, setting boundaries gives you more room to change your identity and enhance your sense of self.

Setting boundaries has noticeable benefits. It allows you to stop yourself from burning out and build a greater sense of self-esteem. It also makes others respect you more. They know that just like them; you need your space. You're no longer a chump and won't be taken for a fool. While you need to continue with your scheduled workouts in the gym, you can still create more room for you to take better care of yourself away from the gym.

Gain a Strong Sense of Self

By setting boundaries for yourself, you'll be in a better position to achieve a strong sense of self. Spending time alone allows you to be kind to yourself and practice self-compassion - especially exercising without any form of entertainment. It's during this time that you'll be able to reassess your values. By now, you already know what you stand for. You know where you stand, and now, you can forgive yourself for falling short previously, standing firm in the belief of where you'd like to see yourself in the future.

Also, by giving yourself more me-time, you'll be able to start making better decisions for yourself. You'll have the courage to say no to others when it's appropriate to do so. This firm stance also positions you to put a stop to the bad habits that prevented you from excelling in the gym previously. Over time, good habits will replace bad habits, some of which are the suggestions I've provided for you in this chapter so far.

Now that you're working toward creating a greater sense of self, let's start moving toward changing your identity for the better.

3.2 Changing Your Identity

It's obvious, isn't it? A change in identity may be in order for a chump who wants to become a champ. But how does Alex or Jay do this?

Before I guide you on how to go about this exercise, I'd like you to spend time reflecting in your journal on no more than one fundamental aspect of yourself that you feel needs to be changed.

For this exercise, you might need to brace yourself for hard truths that highlight ingrained weaknesses, just as you would an opponent in the ring who clearly stands head and shoulders above you in all aspects of the bout.

At the same time, don't let noticeable weaknesses set you back mentally. Treat this reflection exercise as an opportune time to think about your strengths as well, and how you can use these to counter your weaknesses, just as you would to deflect sucker-punches being thrown at you by a Southpaw exponent.

If you could change one thing about yourself, what would it be?

Overcoming Awkwardness

From Muhammad Ali to Ukraine's Klitschko brothers, you'll notice how clumsy and awkward great heavyweights were during their first-ever bouts. But after a few more fights, the joke was on their opponents. Whether through extravagance or honed leadership skills, it did not take these greats long to compose themselves both inside and outside the ring.

Given the true-to-life challenges these great men were faced with, they also had to learn to control their tempers when taunted. Both inside and outside the ring. Both inside and outside the ring, you too can remove yourself from being branded as socially inept by observing the following actions:

- Listen actively when someone is talking to you. Show them that you're interested in what they're saying (even when secretly, you're not) by passing occasional positive remarks.

- Both your verbal responses and your body language are indicative of what is known as positive reinforcement. You're not necessarily agreeing with every word that's being said but are giving your fellow-conversationalist encouragement to continue the conversation.

- When it's appropriate to do so, always ask questions when you're not sure about something that's being said. I always value this response among my trainees down at the gym but continue to remind those still new to our stable that there's no such thing as a stupid question. So too, you should never be afraid to express your opinion, particularly if it's in contrast to what your conversationalist said.

- There's no need to put pressure on yourself when attempting to make the transformation from being awkward to confident when you proceed to practice your newly acquired social skills in low-pressure situations. This would usually include people you trust and who are already familiar with your quirks, and amazingly, don't mind them.

All things being equal, now is also a good time for you to discard all fixed or negative thoughts by replacing it with positive affirmations that are indicative of a growth mindset. Most importantly, whether you're practicing drills in the gym or taking care of yourself away from the gym, practice empathy. That means being kind and patient with yourself, remembering always that if you can take good care of your emotions, you can respond patiently to those you engage with in conversation.

How to Remove Loser Traits

Did you know that South Africa's first democratically elected president was a keen amateur boxer? It did not matter to him that he wasn't good at the sport because he could always remind himself of one of his most famous quotes which states that: "It always seems impossible until it's done".

Like Muhammad Ali and Vitali Klitschko, Nelson Mandela had a winner's mentality. Nearly 30 years of resilient prison life never allowed him to behave like a loser, and instead of berating them, he would always have a kind word of encouragement for those who had practically given up on hope. That said, when it feels like you're getting nowhere in life, the following suggestions will help you to shed your proverbial loser's mentality:

- Take control of your life: You can start by focusing on small, achievable tasks like mastering the medicine ball rather than the punching bag, in order to strengthen your core muscles, rather than perfecting your jabbing skills which may have taken you longer to develop.

- Take the bull by the horns: There's no need to approach someone or a challenging task when you take a direct, immediate approach to tackling a challenge. This, of course, also takes time to develop.

- Take a long-term approach toward changing your attitude: Patience is a virtue, and accept that transformation takes time. It requires continuous patience, resilience, and discipline. You can be successful by visualizing how you'd like to see yourself six to twelve months from the moment you start the process of removing your loser traits.

- Seek help from those who can help you: You'll be interested to note that your qualified or experienced gym trainer can also equip you with life skills and help you with your emotional development.

- Be inspired by others: Whether it's Marvelous Marvin Hagler, Thomas "The Hit Man" Hearns, or Sugar Ray Leonard, Gay or Fury, you can use your favorite boxers as role models. But all good and well to be inspired because it's surely better to follow people who, through discipline, lead by example, both inside the ring and away from it.

How to Apply Winner Traits

Just because the rules of the game require only you to challenge a gargantuan opponent in the ring, doesn't mean that you need to go at it alone. Watching live fights, you will already have seen the advantage of having a man in your corner. Indeed, from a different angle, and with insight, he can see things that you may not be able to see in the heat of the moment.

Your man in the corner is able to provide you with fresh ideas on how you could floor your opponent before he gets the better of you. Your supporter can also help you to focus on areas of your personality that need development or consistency in order to place you at an advantage. Life being hard enough as it is, your man in the corner makes it easier for you to turn what seemed impossible just moments ago into the possible. All of the above might not be possible if you don't keep yourself open to suggestions.

Identity-Based Habits

You are who you are. There are some things about yourself that you can't change. That said, you could seek to tweak those habits that are a reflection of who you are as a sportsman, while at the same time transforming bad habits typical of a chump to healthier habits that will help you think and act like a champ, both inside and outside the ring.

Many of the guys I coach are truly gifted. If not that, they show potential, and they're dedicated to what it takes for them to succeed. I'm happy to say that their influence has rubbed off rather well on Jay, the chump I introduced to you at the beginning of the chapter.

But as far as building up confidence to ask a girl out on a date, there's still work to be done. For many of us, whether as college graduates or divorced middle-aged business owners, there's always room for improvement, no matter how confident we thought we were feeling at any given time. After all, a woman should still be treated as a lady, and your new habits could also help her to elevate her self-esteem as well.

Do you feel that what I've said above applies to you? Do you feel that at this moment in time, you're falling way short of the kind of guy you want to be? Not to worry because the following visualization tools will not only stand you in good stead in terms of raising your confidence levels but also use new levels of confidence to put into practice the habits you previously thought were insurmountable:

- Journal your thoughts on both the positive and negative features of your personality and beliefs. Doing this, focus on your strengths to help motivate you to resiliently challenge the flaws that cause you to lose your discipline to change.

- It becomes easier to do the above when you start asking yourself how you want to feel. Visualizing the sense of well-being you'd like to experience will help you connect more with healthier behavioral patterns that lead to this sense of well-being.

- Challenge your negative self-talk habits by replacing irrational, all-or-nothing thoughts with rational but active engagements, characteristic of the champion's can-do attitude.

Always remember that the champion's mentality believes that nothing is impossible, even during challenging situations. But perhaps this is easier said than done, particularly when the truth of who you are as a sportsman or gentleman who never seems to be able to move from mediocre to promising remains unpalatable.

3.3 Understanding Confidence

"You don't become confident by shouting affirmations in the mirror, but by having a stack of undeniable proof that you are who you say you are. Outwork your self-doubt." - Alex Hormozi

Most fights are won by boxers who have confidence in their abilities. Simply put, those fighters that rarely make it past the first couple of rounds are lacking in confidence. Perhaps that's where you are right now. You don't yet have enough confidence to go the full length of a fight. Or you don't yet have enough confidence to climb in the ring.

Not to worry because that's something that can begin to change as you read your way through this section which reminds you that greater confidence in your abilities and your interactions with others *is* always possible. It ends with a list of things you can do to make confidence-building a regular habit during your daily life.

Experience and Practice

Perhaps regular practice serves as another reminder in the sense that no matter how well-equipped or experienced you are, there are always those moments in your life, and yes, in the ring too, where you could take your eyes off the ball. And before you know it, your opponent has delivered a sucker punch that has the potential to floor you, both figuratively and literally.

That said, practice makes perfect. Think of it this way: In order to build bigger and stronger muscles, there's little left for you to do but continue with your regular reps on the weight training floor. If you want to run faster than you did the last time you competed in a 100-meter dash, you'll be repeating your explosive starts out of the blocks on the track. And if you want to deliver quicker, more explosive punches, no matter how strong you are, you'll be repeating your deliveries on the punching bag.

How to Make Confidence-Building a Habit

In this business-oriented exercise, let me begin by referring you back to your journal. In this exercise, make a list of any successful people—sports and/or business-people—that you can think of, and think hard but not-so-fast about what it took for them to have confidence in their abilities to be successful.

Having read the previous section, the reasons for their success might seem obvious. But there's more to it than meets the eye. Now, after reflecting on this for a few moments, go through the following list of habits and see if any of them appear on your list:

- Get to know yourself: The more you know yourself as a person, the closer you'll be to identifying your flaws, and putting yourself in a position to remove them. But the more you identify with your strengths, the closer you'll come to developing a well-rounded, more confident version of yourself.

- Trust your instincts: Confidence allows you to do this. The more you trust yourself and your values, the more sure you are of your actions. Confidence also allows you to accept that sometimes your instincts may be wrong.

You will, however, be better placed to redress your shortcomings in the event that you've taken a wrong turn.

- Leave your comfort zone: Confidence is not to be confused with complacency. Complacency is indicative of a couldn't-care-less attitude that says that "things will blow over" when you know full well that extricating yourself from a challenging situation requires work.

- Build up evidence to challenge yourself: For all the times that you disappoint yourself even further by delaying outcomes through negatively influenced inaction, challenge yourself with a positive version of "what-if" possibilities. In this case, you'll be reminding yourself that all things are possible if you take action.

- Take full responsibility: All things are possible if you take full responsibility for your actions, particularly when you've made mistakes. Confidence also teaches you humility. Humility allows you to acknowledge your shortcomings, and to apologize readily if they've negatively impacted others.

Confidence also teaches you to know your limits. But if that's the case, why does it look like our role models are always pushing themselves to the limits? How does it come to be that they always seem to get away with murder, figuratively speaking, of course?

3.4 Pushing Your Limits

It is in the nature of the sport to push yourself to the limit. Sadly, this never-say-die attitude has been the downfall of many boxers, many of whose careers have ended prematurely. Let me explain: Good to know if you have it within you to push yourself to the limit. But at the same time, in order for you to get to this point without injuring or endangering yourself, you'd have to know your limits as well.

It also takes discipline. It takes discipline to restrain yourself, whether you're faced with a confrontation at work, endeavoring to do some last-minute cramming for an exam, or resisting the urge to have that slice of chocolate cake you have been craving for days.

In this section, I'll take you through what is necessary to develop discipline. I'll motivate you in this direction by highlighting the benefits that discipline brings you. But knowing that it's possible to push yourself to the limit, you might be impatient to learn what it may take. That said, it's still necessary to know your limits. After all, no matter who you are in life, you can only push yourself so far, and no further.

What It Takes

Truth be told, to the rest of us, it only *looks* like these champions are pushing themselves to the limit. The fact of the matter is that some of them have been practicing their acquired or honed skills for a lifetime. But if they are pushing themselves to the limit—without injuring themselves in the process—they've more than likely been doing so with discipline.

True champions are more than willing to regularly discipline themselves, knowing full well that it has its benefits. They don't know this from hindsight; they know this from experience. And with experience, you'll experience the following benefits as well:

- *You'll have more confidence in your abilities.*

- *You'll experience improved strength, health, and fitness.*

- *You'll be better focused and more resilient whenever you're faced with adversity.*

- *Whether in the gym or at work, knowing that you can achieve more with less, you'll be more productive in all areas of your life.*

But really, is it worth pushing yourself to the limit? And apart from wanting to achieve results, why do we choose to push ourselves to the limit?

Whether it's logical or not, we believe that by pushing ourselves to the limit, improvements may be possible, come hell or high weather. We've even deluded ourselves with the champion's mentality, believing that to restrain ourselves or stop what we're doing to re-assess what we're doing is similar to quitting. In the process, we forget too easily that there's also value in quitting while we're ahead.

We may also have forgotten that the "no pain, no gain" mantra could be counterproductive to our efforts. Even so, those who are able to distinguish between pain and suffering may have a point in the sense that actual or literal pain might be a disciplined reflection of what we need to go through in order to achieve results, while suffering is a negative reflection of what we've been through to achieve our objectives, particularly when they weren't met.

While rewarding ourselves for a job well done is mindful, we're prepared to delay gratification until the job's done, sometimes without any pauses in between. Surely, this is hardly healthy. Even so, positive, determined sportsmen are somehow able to ignore negative perceptions and focus on their goals.

Understand Your Limits

The reality is that no matter what it is you wish for or need to do, nothing of substance comes to you easily. Wanting something is all good and well but in order to obtain that something you're craving, you have to work toward obtaining it. That said, the positive mindset allows you to accept that there will be a period of pain and suffering, safe in the knowledge that such pain and suffering is well worth the trouble when you're finally rewarded.

Even so, an appreciation of what you can put yourself through is needed. It is this appreciation that helps you to understand that no matter how good a boxer or husband you are, what you can put yourself through has its limits. There is only so much a man can do.

Knowing your limits is healthy because it allows you to plan for the worst, always hoping for the best. Allowing yourself to be vulnerable in the face of adversity should never be regarded as a sign of weakness. Rather, it is a sign of strength.

How to Develop Discipline

Knowing how vulnerable you are as a man also provides you with the impetus to become better disciplined. This, of course, also requires proper planning. Let me assure you that by including the following steps in your mental preparation, you will succeed in developing the required discipline:

- *Be honest with yourself about your limitations.*

- *Be clear about the goals you have in mind.*

- *Break down your goals into smaller achievable chunks.*

- *Prioritize your goals and be as thorough as possible when planning for them.*

- *Make yourself accountable to others.*

Whether it's your coach, teammate, supervisor, or workplace colleagues, your future accountability partners can help you monitor your progress by providing you with honest feedback. It's also as my line editors sometimes like to remind me: It's helpful to have a third eye.

How to Develop Realistic Habits That Won't Break

It is like having a sponsor at a downtown AA meeting. He will be monitoring your progress but won't be watching you like a hawk. He won't castigate you either if you suffer a relapse and break your pledge. Rather, like a dove, he will offer you reassurance, comfort, and support.

The above list of disciplinary tactics recommends that you start with goals that are achievable. The same goes for habits that you don't want to break, meaning that you'll be starting off with a small habit-forming task that can be repeated easily. Once you've managed to create an unbroken chain of repeated events, you can start thinking about practicing the next habit.

Make sure that it's easy for you to stay true to these habits, you'll want them to coincide. They must make sense to you, and they must be necessary. It's like washing and drying the dishes after dinner. While you could conceivably leave these dishes to stand in their rack overnight, it would surely be better to pack them away once they're dry as there won't be any dishes for you to pack away the next day.

What are known as stack habits also make it easier for you to break into new habits. It also helps if you're able to remove obstacles or impediments that stand in the way of your habits. For instance, you'll want to cut out a drinking night at your local sports bar, knowing full well that you have a five-mile run to get through the following morning.

See this more as a compromise. After all, if it's a championship fight or NBA final you're using as an excuse to go drinking, you can surely watch the fight or game at home. That said, treat yourself to an alcohol-free, calorie-light beer as a reward for your discipline.

3.5 Overcoming Setbacks

Earlier, I mentioned former South African president, Nelson Mandela. I mentioned too that he was a hapless amateur boxer when he was young. But I never mentioned the enormity of the amount of setbacks he had to endure throughout his life. It led me to think that our setbacks must surely pale into insignificance when we think about what challenges he had to face.

Mandela was also philosophical about these setbacks. If it wasn't for them, he would not have become the great statesman that he was during his last years. More importantly, he could learn from these setbacks. And no matter what setbacks you're faced with, you can learn too. It's also as the saying goes: "It's not about how hard you can hit, it's about how hard you can get hit and keep moving forward."

That said, it would seem that sometimes in life, setbacks can be good for us. But how can this be? How can additional burdens that no one wanted be of any help?

Sometimes, Setbacks Are Good for You

According to Harvard Business Review researchers, people who've endured setbacks are more likely to reassess their goals and career-oriented aspirations. Long after they've recovered from their setbacks, the researchers found, they would continue with this ongoing habit of reassessment. Having learned from their setbacks, these people became more resilient and focused on new growth-oriented paths of learning, all in the interest of either avoiding a future setback or managing it better than ever before.

Keeping Track of Your Setbacks

On the surface, it may seem corny to you but I believe that it's a good idea to keep track of your setbacks, just as you would your new habits or training requirements. But it goes without saying that, ideally, you'll want to be in a positive frame of mind when you reflect on any future setbacks, just like Mandela did back then. Positive feedback from your setbacks is achieved when you acknowledge and accept them.

Keeping track of your setbacks is indicative of reflecting on them. Pausing for thought, you're positioning yourself to adjust plans going forward, to either avoid future setbacks or better manage them. It goes without saying that this tracking process should provide you with the space to learn from these setbacks, whether you're responsible for them or circumstances beyond your control have been the root cause of them.

Ultimately, plans and strategies may need to change but your end-goals don't need to. Now, it's just a matter of achieving them.

3.6 Strength in Numbers

You stand a better chance of reaching your goals when you've gained the support of others. A promising high school kid from the suburbs who has the full support of his parents has a greater chance of achieving success than another kid who, with similar aspirations, is faced with challenges typical of a life lived in the so-called projects, and with no parental support to boot.

And I've yet to see any boxer, whether an amateur contender or an Olympic athlete, achieve success without the help of a coach. Traditionally, the Olympic athlete will be traveling to the games as a member of a team. It is rare to see this happening otherwise.

Teamwork provides you with motivational support alongside critical evaluations, particularly when you're in no position to provide them yourself. And of course, teamwork is not confined to sports. It applies to everyday life as well, particularly in the workplace. An effective team led by an equally effective team leader or supervisor is a lot more productive and motivated than a team led by a proverbial boss who merely dishes out orders, expecting his subordinates to comply with them.

Why We're Better in a Team

Lest I remind you, boxing is not an individual sport. It is a team sport. Boxers with full support in their corner of the ring function better. But let's assume that your interest in boxing goes no further than an enjoyable pastime designed to help keep you fit and strong. Boxing goes further because it's a sport that can teach you to become a valuable and productive team player.

Apart from promoting fitness and teamwork, boxing can help you to improve your confidence and concentration levels, alongside teaching you to become better disciplined. Boxing benefits our students by getting them fit, teaching them teamwork, anger management, and discipline, and improving their confidence and concentration.

Use the Boxing Gym

For boxers, the training environment is ideal for developing the ability to become a cooperative team player. The collaborative spirit that forms part of the gym's atmosphere is a positive contributing factor toward improving performance levels. What's also great about being a gym member is that you're more than likely going to be part of a competitive environment. While human beings are social creatures by nature, potential champs cannot rid themselves of their competitive streak.

Moreover, while egos may be bruised when experiencing defeat in full view of others, teamwork in the gym helps to build character. You may watch others who are better than you without needing to be jealous of their prowess when you learn with and from them. And just as the sport has its rules, being part of a boxing team requires you to follow a list of prescribed rules as well.

3.7 Champions Mentality

If you don't box and see no chance of playing competitive sport in the future, other than keeping fit through regular gym visits and road work, you still have it within you to become a champion. You can be a champ in everyday life, always doing what is right and what you believe is right. As a cooperative and productive team player in the workplace, you have what it takes to become a leader as well.

You don't need to be the leader of the team as Wayne Gretzky was. You can simply lead by example, just like the LA Lakers' LeBron James still does today. A champion communicates well too. While he's a good listener, he won't necessarily bore you to tears with long stories. A simple yes or no may do for the champion communicator who addresses you clearly and directly.

And while the non-sporting champ will do everything within his powers to avoid getting into a fight, he's not afraid of conflict.

All things being equal—and whether you box or not—life's pretty good for you when you're a champ. Life's pretty good *to* you as well. This has nothing to do with you being the luckiest man alive. Rather, it has everything to do with the effort you're prepared to put into disciplining yourself, keeping yourself mentally and physically fit and strong, and continuing to develop your character.

Developing a Strong Sense of Self

I say this with a great sense of positivity but sometimes a coach like me has no alternative but to focus on psychological aspects of the sport being played. A coach like me not only needs to nurture and love those he trains, particularly those who are battling to shed their chumpy scales, but to teach them to nurture and love themselves as well. And I like to tell them that life can be good for you but only if they do something about making this possible.

Being able to love yourself allows you to live the life you choose for yourself. Helping you to do this is the development of a strong sense of self, which can be achieved if you adopt the following actions:

- *Develop your confidence levels to allow you to be comfortable in your own skin.*

- *Develop yourself further by challenging yourself.*

- *Allow yourself to be vulnerable sometimes so that others can see you at an intimate level.*

- *Don't let others define who you are as an individual.*

The Champ Knows How to Set Boundaries

Others should not be allowed to dictate how you should live your life, just as long as you're staying true to your values and doing what is right. Others cannot be allowed to set your boundaries because as a champ, that's a task that you'll master over time. At the same time, you need to be realistic about the challenges you're faced with, so much so that if it means pulling out of a fight, then so be it.

I mean this figuratively in the sense that it's not worth risking your mind and body in a fight you're not prepared for. This, however, does not mean you're afraid of conflict. You're not a coward. You can, however, prepare yourself well for change, by working through all the strategies that have been provided in this chapter to help you build your confidence and develop a strong sense of character that is also indicative of who you are as an individual.

Whether you've allowed others to help you or prepared your own self-help plan, stick to the plan that's been created for you. It's only when you've tested it and experienced its results that you can justify going back to the drawing board to reassess what you've been doing if the results haven't gone the way you anticipated.

The Champ Is Not Afraid of Conflict

It's a case of stating the obvious, isn't it? While the wise champ will do everything within his power to avoid a conflict, he's not afraid of it. He knows that he can deal with a conflict if it's unavoidable because he's prepared himself for that moment. In the context of *Boxing From Chump to Champ*, the champ might be a pugilist by trade but will choose to resort to words rather than fisticuffs to resolve a conflict in order to prevent it from spiraling out of control.

At the height of a confrontation, the champ will remain composed while addressing the issues at hand. He avoids personal attacks and will not assign blame to his opponent. He can get to know what his antagonist might be going through because he listens carefully to what is being said. As an active listener, the champ listens carefully to what his aggressor is trying to communicate.

The Champ Always Gets the Job Done

The champ works toward avoiding last-minute jobs. Not because he doesn't want to work but because it's far more efficient to prepare tasks ahead of time, and complete them on time. While the champ may have no illusions about what challenges he may be faced with while endeavoring to complete his tasks, he has more than enough confidence in his abilities to meet these challenges.

As far as the champ is concerned, life remains a race to the finish line. But as a champ, he's in no hurry to finish the race. After all, life is good for the champ, and why not prolong it to enjoy it to the full.

Conclusion

Thank you for making it through to the end of *Boxing From Chump to Champ*, I hope it was informative and able to provide you with all of the tools you need to achieve the results you desire. As a boxing coach for many years now, I have had the pleasure of teaching numerous students who want to become a better version of themselves. However, training people in person limits the number of people I can break through to. This is why I am excited to be able to write a book, which can be enjoyed by people all over the world. Whether you are in a major city or a small rural town in the middle of nowhere, you can be introduced to the world of boxing and glean from the wisdom I have gained. This knowledge comes from my own mentors and students alike.

As a trainer and fan of boxing, I am proud to have this sport be a part of my life. Not only have I seen people get fit and healthy, but I also witnessed them improving in every area of their lives. In many cases, they became a whole new person. This is because boxing not only strengthens the body but strengthens the mind. The skills you learn in this diverse sport can be carried with you in every area of your life. There are countless examples in real life where boxing saved someone from going on a dark path. It is a sport that teaches strength, discipline, hard work, integrity, and goal setting. My hope and expectations are that you become a better person in your own way.

My promise to you was that you would learn about the many fundamentals of boxing and realize the many benefits that come from the sport. I believe the topics and information I have provided are a great starting point for you as you enter the sport in whatever capacity you decide. If you plan on competing, I wish you well. If you don't, then I hope you got something positive from this book.

The next step is to start using the knowledge I have provided and begin practicing the various techniques immediately. You can train in all of these from the comfort of your home, and do not have to join a gym unless you choose to. Practice is what makes perfect, and you must practice these techniques over and over again to become comfortable with them. This is just the beginning. If you plan on making boxing a major part of your life, then, eventually, you will have to go beyond the confines of this book and keep learning something new. I have faith that you will do very well. Thank you for taking the time to learn something I am passionate about.

References

Join the Facebook Community. https://www.facebook.com/groups/chumptochamp

Ahmed, K. (2023, January 25). *There is no such thing as "weakness". It is only a lack of self-awareness.* LinkedIn. https://www.linkedin.com/pulse/thing-weakness-only-lack-self-awareness-kashif-ahmed/

Ameer, M. (2023, April 21). *How to identify your personal strengths and weaknesses.* LinkedIn. https://www.linkedin.com/pulse/how-identify-your-personal-strengths-weaknesses-muslim-ameer/

Boyes, A. (2020, December 31). *6 tips for when you feel like a loser at life.* Psychology Today. https://www.psychologytoday.com/us/blog/in-practice/202012/6-tips-when-you-feel-loser-life

Cooper, B. (2016, January 28). *How I became a morning person, read 5x more books and learned a new language in a year.* Buffer. https://buffer.com/resources/building-habits/

Derreumaux, C. (2024, January 21). *How to positively handle a setback.* https://www.cyrilderreumaux.com/blog/how-to-positively-handle-a-setback

11 habits of confident people. (n.d). Small Business BC. https://smallbusinessbc.ca/article/11-habits-of-confident-people/

Fonda, P. (n.d). *How teamwork can improve your physical performance*. Velites. https://en.velitessport.com/teamwork-can-improve-physical-performance/

Foster, R. (2024, February 8). *Focus on your 'who': why identity is a powerful tool for behavior change and healthy habits*. Hinge Health. https://www.hingehealth.com/resources/articles/identity-and-habits/#:~:text=Visualize%20Your%20Future%20Self&text=Focus%20on%20your%20%E2%80%9Cfuture%20self,in%20alignment%20with%20that%20identity.

Hailey, L. (2023, October 30). *8 signs you're socially inept & how to overcome awkwardness*. Science of People. https://www.scienceofpeople.com/socially-inept/#how-to-stop-being-socially-inept

How to become more disciplined: 7 tips for self-discipline. (n.d). Calm. https://www.calm.com/blog/how-to-become-more-disciplined

Kutscher, G. & Mayrhofer, W. (2023, December 1). *Research: setbacks can actually boost your career*. Harvard Business Review. https://hbr.org/2023/12/research-setbacks-can-actually-boost-your-career#:~:text=We%20found%20that%20people%20who%2

7d%20had%20a%20setback%20were,who%20had%20never%20faced%20adversity.

Perry, E. (2022, September 14). *What is self-awareness and how to develop it.* BetterUp. https://www.betterup.com/blog/what-is-self-awareness

Price, A. (n.d). *Learning to love yourself: how to develop a strong sense of self.* https://amberaprice.com/building-a-strong-sense-of-self/

Rajora, P. (2023, March 10). *It always seems impossible until it's done.* LinkedIn. https://www.linkedin.com/pulse/always-seems-impossible-until-its-done-preeti-rajora/

7 successful conflict management skills every leader needs to know. (2023, October 20). IT By Design. https://www.linkedin.com/pulse/7-successful-conflict-management-skills-every-leader-needs/

Sharanu, C. (2024, May 27). *How to be a winner: 10 tips to achieve success.* Discover. https://discover.hubpages.com/business/How-To-Be-A-Winner

6 tips to set boundaries with difficult people. (2024, February 20). Sharp. https://www.sharp.com/health-news/6-tips-to-set-boundaries-with-difficult-people

Why Boxing?. (n.d). The Boxing Academy. https://www.theboxingacademy.co.uk/about-us/why-boxing

Woods, A. (2021, December 20). *Why can some people push themselves to the limit while others can't?*. Flux. https://www.fluxmagazine.com/some-people-push-themselves-to-the-limit/

Wooll, M. (2022, February 14). *Become a pro at asking for feedback (and receiving it)*. BetterUp. https://www.betterup.com/blog/how-to-ask-for-and-receive-feedback#:~:text=Only%20ask%20for%20feedback%20from,hear%20from%20others%20as%20well.

Wooll, M. (2022, February 25). *360-degree feedback: definition, benefits, and examples*. BetterUp. https://www.betterup.com/blog/360-degree-feedback

4 Drills To Improve Your Boxing Defense. (2018, July 3). Evolve MMA Singapore. https://evolve-mma.com/blog/4-drills-to-improve-your-boxing-defense/
5 Common Mistakes To Avoid When Throwing Hooks In Boxing. (2018, July 17). Evolve MMA Singapore. https://evolve-mma.com/blog/5-common-mistakes-to-avoid-when-throwing-hooks-in-boxing/
5 Important Aspects Of The Mental Side Of Boxing. (2018, June 13). Evolve MMA Singapore. https://evolve-mma.com/blog/5-important-aspects-of-the-mental-side-of-boxing/
admin. (2017, December 7). *Boxing Footwork Fundamentals*. The Ultimate Boxing Experience. https://precisionstriking.com/boxing-footwork-tips-fundamentals/

Basic boxing combinations for beginners. (2019, March 20). Law of the Fist. https://lawofthefist.com/basic-boxing-combinations-for-beginners/

Best Post-Workout Stretching Exercises | The Boxing Club. (2015, February 17). The Boxing Club. https://www.theboxingclub.net/blog/best-post-workout-stretching-exercises

Boxing styles and techniques. (n.d.). Boxing Wiki. Retrieved June 20, 2020, from https://boxing.fandom.com/wiki/Boxing_styles_and_technique

C. (2019, March 6). *A Guide to Perfecting the Boxers Diet | Superprof.* The Superprof Blog - UK. https://www.superprof.co.uk/blog/what-is-a-boxers-diet/

Chen, J. (2019, October 24). *How to Throw a Punch Correctly.* Lifehacker. https://lifehacker.com/how-to-throw-a-punch-correctly-5829523

Conway, T. (2019, July 3). *Tyson Fury Talks Mental Health Struggles, Reveals He Was on the Verge of Suicide.* Bleacher Report. https://bleacherreport.com/articles/2839648-tyson-fury-talks-mental-health-struggles-reveals-he-was-on-the-verge-of-suicide

FITNESS COMPONENTS. (n.d.). Art of Boxing. Retrieved June 29, 2020, from http://boxingkent00.tripod.com/id5.html

Gunnars, K. B. (2018, July 11). *The 20 Most Weight-Loss-Friendly Foods on The Planet.* Healthline. https://www.healthline.com/nutrition/20-most-weight-loss-friendly-foods

Lehane, A. (2020, May 10). *How Important Is Running For Boxing? Everything You Need To Know.* Boxing Addicts.

http://boxingaddicts.com/how-important-is-running-for-boxing/

N, J. (2012, October 21). *Advanced Slipping Technique, PART 2 – Body Movement.* How to Box | ExpertBoxing. https://expertboxing.com/how-to-throw-a-jab

N, J. (2014b, March 30). *How to Fight a Southpaw.* How to Box | ExpertBoxing. https://expertboxing.com/how-to-throw-an-uppercut

N, J. (2019, January 20). *How to Fight a Southpaw.* How to Box | ExpertBoxing. https://expertboxing.com/boxing-defense-techniques

Stinson, A. (2017, July 13). *5 Boxing Workouts At Home Without Equipment That Will Feel Just As Good As Hitting The Bag.* Elite Daily. https://www.elitedaily.com/wellness/5-workouts-boxing-gym-can-easily-done-comfort-home/2017371

Types of Boxing Stances & Style Explained. (2017, September 15). RDX Sports Blog. http://blogs.rdxsports.com/boxing-stances/

What Are The Different Types of Punch Bags And What Are They For? (2018, May 16). Boxfit Blog. https://www.boxfituk.com/blog/what-are-the-different-types-of-punch-bags-and-what-are-they-for

www.ingramcontent.com/pod-product-compliance
Lightning Source LLC
Chambersburg PA
CBHW030450100526
44580CB00002B/60